Malcolm Shuttleworth
Englisch, aber richtig!

Malcolm Shuttleworth

Englisch, aber richtig!

Der 20-Punkte-Plan
zum Verlernen der häufigsten Fehler

Mit zahlreichen Illustrationen des Autors

Anaconda

Die Deutsche Nationalbibliothek verzeichnet diese Publikation
in der Deutschen Nationalbibliografie; detaillierte bibliografische Daten
sind im Internet unter http://dnb.d-nb.de abrufbar.

Umschlagmotiv: shutterstock/Thinglass
Umschlaggestaltung: Druckfrei. Dagmar Herrmann, Bad Honnef
Satz und Layout: www.paque.de
Printed in Czech Republic 2018
ISBN 978-3-7306-0640-7
www.anacondaverlag.de
info@anacondaverlag.de

Vorwort

Man muss kein Sprachgenie sein, um gut Englisch zu sprechen oder zu schreiben. Das Wichtigste ist, keine dummen Fehler zu machen. Die Vermeidung von typischen Fehlern kann den Unterschied zwischen gutem oder schlechtem Englisch bedeuten. Dies ist ein 20-Punkte-Plan, um sein Englisch zu verbessern.

Das Buch kann auf zwei Arten verwendet werden:

1. Wie ein normales Lehrbuch

Lies die Informationen in jedem Abschnitt sorgfältig durch, mach die Fortschrittstests am Ende jedes Abschnitts und überprüfe die Antworten im Lösungsteil am Ende des Buches.

Wenn die Ergebnisse gut sind, kann man zum nächsten Kapitel übergehen. Wenn die Ergebnisse nicht gut sind, sollte der Abschnitt erneut gelesen und der Fortschrittstest wiederholt werden, bevor es zum nächsten Abschnitt weitergeht.

2. Als Nachschlagewerk

Unsicher, wie man ›will future‹ benutzt? Schau dir einfach den entsprechenden Abschnitt an (Point 15). Nicht sicher, was der Unterschied zwischen Adjektiv und Adverb ist? Der Abschnitt ›Get to grips with adjectives and adverbs‹ (Point 6) hilft weiter.

Lies die Regeln genau durch, überprüfe deinen Fortschritt anhand der Test und stelle fest, ob du besser geworden bist.

Progress tests

Die Fortschrittstests können nach jedem Abschnitt durchgeführt werden. Die Noten sollten am Ende des Buches überprüft und die Anweisungen und Bemerkungen zur Kenntnis genommen werden.

Inhalt

Point 1

Improve your spelling

Eine der schnellsten Möglichkeiten, sein geschriebenes Englisch zu verbessern, ist die Verbesserung der eigenen Rechtschreibung.

Dies sind die häufigsten Rechtschreibfehler, die gemacht werden.

1. K

Die goldene Regel

Wenn es im Deutschen ein ***k*** *ist, ist es im Englischen ein* ***c****!*

Beispiele

Aspekt	–	aspect
Defekt	–	defect
akzeptabel	–	acceptable
Kalendar	–	calendar
Krokodil	–	crocodile
Kaktus	–	cactus
Katze	–	cat
Kamm	–	comb
Kommando	–	commando
Kommentar	–	comment
Kritiker	–	critic

2. E

Ein weiterer großer Fehler ist es, das **e** am Ende bestimmter Wörter zu vergessen.

before	not	befor
because	not	becaus
decide	not	decid
satellite	not	satellite
prize	not	priz

und auch **-ble …**

sensible	not	~~sensibel~~
example	not	~~exampel~~
possible	not	~~possibel~~

3. He/she/it, ein s muss mit – the third person singular (he/she/it)

… aber ganz so einfach ist das nicht!
Um diesen Fehler zu vermeiden, muss man alle dazugehörigen Regeln lernen.

s or es?

In vielen Fällen genügt es, dem Verb nur ein **-s** hinzuzufügen, aber sei vorsichtig. Dies gilt nicht, wenn die Verben auf o, sh, ch, ss, x enden! Dann **-es**.

Beispiele

nach o

do – I do, you do, we do — he do**es**, she do**es**, it do**es**
go – I go, you go, they go — he go**es**, she go**es**, it go**es**

nach sh

wash – I wash, you wash, we wash — he wash**es**, she wash**es**, it wash**es**
mash – I mash, you mash, we mash — he mash**es**, she mash**es**, it mash**es**

nach ch

watch – I watch, you watch, we watch — he watch**es**, she watch**es**, it watch**es**
catch – I catch, you catch, we catch — he catch**es**, she catch**es**, it catch**es**

nach ss

cross – I cross, you cross, we cross — he cross**es**, she cross**es**, it cross**es**
toss – I toss, you toss, we toss — he toss**es**, she toss**es**, it toss**es**

nach x

box – I box, you box, we box — he box**es**, she box**es**, it box**es**
toss – I toss, you toss, we toss — he toss**es**, she toss**es**, it toss**es**

Plural nouns
Diese es-Regel gilt auch für Substantive im Plural!

nach o
One hero – two hero**es**
One potato – two potato**es**

nach sh
One crash – two crash**es**
One rash – two rash**es**

nach ch
One watch – two watch**es**
One match – two match**es**

nach ss
One cross – two cross**es**
One boss – two boss**es**

nach x
One box – two box**es**
One fox – two fox**es**

4. Wörter, die auf -y enden

Verben, die auf **-y** enden, haben eine Reihe von Regeln für sich. (Es ist wichtig, diese Regeln zu lernen, denn dies ist eine weitere, äußerst beliebte Fehlerquelle.)

a. Verben, die auf -y enden in der dritten Person Singular (er/sie/es)
Wenn dem y ein Vokal vorangestellt ist (a, e, i, o, u), hänge einfach ein -s an das Wort.

play	–	I play, you play, play	he play**s**, she play**s**, it play**s**
lay	–	I lay, you, lay, we lay	he lay**s**, she lay**s**, it lay**s**
pay	–	I pay, you pay, we pay	he pay**s**, she pay**s**, it pay**s**
say	–	I say, you say, they say	he say**s**, she say**s**, it say**s**

b. Aber wenn dem y ein Konsonant (b, c, d, f usw.) vorangestellt ist, wird statt -ys immer -ies verwendet.

try	–	I try, you, try, we try	he tr**ies**, she tr**ies**, it tr**ies**
cry	–	I cry, you, cry, we cry	he cr**ies**, she cr**ies**, it cr**ies**
fry	–	I fry, you fry, we fry	he fr**ies**, she fr**ies**, it fr**ies**
fly	–	I fly, you fly, we fly	he fl**ies**, she fl**ies**, it fl**ies**

5. Doubling the last letter

Folge diesen vier goldenen Regeln:

a. Consonant-vowel-consonant ending (C-V-C) = *double the last letter:*

Diese Regel gilt für reguläre Verben, die eine Silbe lang sind und die in der ing-Form des Verbs vorliegen.

verb	**past tense**	**-ing form**
I s**hop** every day.	I sho**pp**ed yesterday.	I am sho**pp**ing.
I c**hop** firewood.	I cho**pp**ed firewood on Friday.	I am cho**pp**ing firewood.
I **nap** in the afternoon.	I na**pp**ed yesterday.	Granddad is na**pp**ing.

b. Wenn das Verb *nicht* auf Konsonant-Vokal-Konsonant endet, einfach -ed oder -ing anhängen:

verb	**past tense**	**-ing form**
I e**arn** money.	I ear**ned** money last year.	I am **earning** money.
I l**ook** at the birds.	I loo**ked** at the birds last night.	I am **looking** at the moon.

c. Bei regelmäßigen Verben, die auf -e enden, fügst du in der Vergangenheitsform einfach -d an:

I danc**e**	–	I danc**ed**
we bake	–	we bak**ed**

d. Bei der ing-Form, wird das e ausgelassen:

I danc**e**	–	I am **dancing**
I bak**e**	–	I am **baking**

6. Most misspelt words

Dies sind die am häufigsten falsch geschriebenen Wörter auf Englisch. Die Problembereiche sind fettgedruckt.

correct spelling	spelling tips	common misspelling
a**cc**o**mm**odation	double c, double m	acomodation/ accomodation
a**dd**ress	double d	adress
arg**u**ment	spelt without ue	arguement
believ**e**	-e at the end	believ
b**us**iness	double s, not spelt with ui	buisness
calend**a**r	starts with c	kalendar
c**e**m**e**t**e**ry	three e's	cemetary
colleag**ue**	ue at the end	college
con**science**	not spelt like it sounds	conscious
definit**e**ly	spelt with two e's	definitly
disa**pp**oint	one s, double p	disapoint
emba**rr**a**ss**	double r, double s	embarras
enviro**n**ment	spelt with an n	enviroment
f**or**ty	not spelt with ou	fourty
h**ei**ght	ei, not ie	hieght
gover**n**ment	spelt with an n	goverment
happen**ed**	regular verb, spelt with -ed	happend
immediat**e**ly	an e before the ly	immediatly
lib**r**ary	two r's	libary
perso**nn**el	double n	personal
politic**ian**	-ian at the end	politican
Portug**u**ese	capital p, two u's	portugese
po**ss**e**ss**ion	double -s twice	possesion
real**l**y	double l	realy
rec**ei**ve	ei not ie	recieve
sep**a**rate	a in the middle	seperate
tr**u**ly	not splet with ue	truely
w**ei**rd	ei not ie	wierd

Erinnerung

1. Mache den Test.
2. Überprüfe die Antworten und Anweisungen am Ende des Buches.

Point 1 – Progress test
Improve your spelling

1. Doing business in the global market

Find the mistakes in the two texts.

One aspekt of doing business that I don't enjoy is the speed at which things have to be done. Befor we had satellits, e-mail and smart phones, life was much easier. Nowadays we have to decid on the spot, make quick decisions and simply do not have time to think. My colleague do a lot of business overseas, I deal with the German market. He go to America quite a lot, in fact he cross the Atlantic nearly every month. I usually flies on business about once a year, but he flys regularly. But I can't complain. At the moment I am earning a lot of money, which is lucky becaus my wife's hobby is shoping.

Time flys

Last week I looked at my kalendar and couldn't believ it was nearly Christmas – time flys. It only seems like last week that I was on my summer holiday. It was great to go danceing every night, naping by the pool in the afternoon and runing on the beach every morning. I went fishhing twice, even tried a little bit of divving.

2. Most misspelled words

Underline the mistake and write the correct spelling on the right.

Mistakes	Corrected words
1. Its raining again.	
2. Your so boring.	
3. They don't like there teacher.	
4. I didn't acheive much at school.	
5. I will definitly see you tomorrow.	
6. The course was good in the begining.	

7. I don't belive you.	
8. Will we get there befor six?	
9. He has no respekt for his teachers.	
10. Buisness has been really bad this year.	
11. He is nearly fourty years old.	
12. Do you know what happend?	
13. I realy don't know.	
14. Therefor we need a new computer.	
15. I truely hate my boss.	
16. I don't like politicans.	
17. My collegue is very lazy.	
18. That is a seperate issue.	
19. Write the appointment on the calender.	
20. Our goverment is terrible.	

Point 2

Use the right verbs

Bei Verben werden zwei grundlegende Fehler gemacht:

1. Das falsche Verb wird verwendet.
2. Das Verb wird in der falschen Zeit verwendet.

1. The right verbs

(Die richtigen Verben)

Dies ist eine grundlegende Anleitung zur Vermeidung der häufigsten Fehler bei der Auswahl des zu verwendenden Verbs. Diese wichtigen Fakten sollten berücksichtigt werden:

- **Do** beschreibt in der Regel eine Handlung, die mit Arbeit verbunden ist. (I **do** my work, job, homework, housework, gardening, shopping.)
- **Make** wird hauptsächlich für die Herstellung von Dingen verwendet. (I **make** a cake, I'll **make** a cup of coffee, shall we **make** pizza?)
- **Drive** wird für Fahrzeuge benutzt (man kann einen Bus, ein Auto, ein Taxi, einen Lastwagen usw. fahren).
- **Ride** wird für Fortbewegungsmittel benutzt, auf denen man sitzt (**ride** a horse, a pony, a motorbike, a scooter, a donkey, etc.). **Achtung!** Ein Bus wird normalerweise nicht selbst gefahren – das darf nur der Busfahrer! Für Passagiere gilt: **Take** the bus, **travel/ride** by bus, train, etc.
- **Go on** or **take a holiday**
- **Go on** a bike trip, a sight-seeing trip or a business trip
- **Listen to** music (aktives Zuhören). But you **hear** a noise (passive Geräuschwahrnehmung).
- **Make** a mistake
- **Do** sport
- **Do** business with another person/business/country
- **Have** a party. You can also **throw** a party.
- **Spend** money on something/someone but **donate** money (to a charity, etc.)

- **Stand up** when you don't want to sit down anymore, but **get up** in the morning.
- **Take** a photo
- **Watch** sport or films

2. The right tense

(Verwendung der korrekten Zeitform und Beachtung von Signalwörtern)

Ein weiterer häufiger Fehler ist die Verwendung der falschen Zeitform. Die goldene Regel lautet:

Das richtige **VERB** ist nur die halbe Miete – zweimal denken!

Sobald das richtige Verb gefunden ist, muss es mit der richtigen Zeitform kombiniert werden. Hier helfen Signalwörter.

Was ist ein Signalwort?

Ein Signalwort ist ein Wort, das hilft, die richtige Zeitform zu finden, da es nur mit einer bestimmten Zeitform verwendet wird.

a. Most common signal words for the simple present

(Die häufigsten Signalwörter für die einfache Gegenwart)

– always, never, sometimes, every (week, day, summer, …)

Diese Worte dienen alle als Signale für die einfache Gegenwart. Mit dieser Zeitform werden Handlungen beschrieben, die regelmäßig oder häufig gemacht werden, z. B. jeden Tag.

Beispiele

I **always** play football on Monday.

I **never** go swimming.

He **sometimes** eats fish on Friday.

Every summer we go to Spain.

I get up for work at six o'clock **every day**.

b. Most common signal words for the simple past

(Die häufigsten Signalwörter für die einfache Vergangenheit)

– yesterday, last week, last year, in 1998, two weeks ago

Diese Worte sind Signale für die einfache Vergangenheit, die verwendet wird, um abgeschlossene Handlungen zu beschreiben.

Beispiele

I went to Spain **last summer**.

He went to the cinema **last night**.

I drove my wife to the airport **yesterday**.

We visited my daughter **two weeks ago**.

c. Most common signal words for the present progressive

(Die häufigsten Signalwörter für die Verlaufsform der Gegenwart)

– is/are/am, ing-Form des Verbs, now, at the moment

Wenn **is/are/am** verwendet wird, ist dies das Signal für die Verwendung der Verlaufsform -ing. Die Verlaufsform beschreibt Handlungen, die jetzt gerade im Moment passieren.

Die goldene Regel

is/are/am nicht ohne **-ing** verwenden.

-ing nicht ohne is/are/am verwenden.

I am

you/we/they are + verb + -ing

he/she/it

I **am working** now.

I **am going** to school at the moment.

She **is talking** to Paul now.

d. Negatives

(Verneinungen)

don't/doesn't/didn't sind Signalwörter für die Verwendung des *Infinitivs* – die Grundform des Verbs:

I **don't** play football.

We **don't** play football.

He **doesn't** play football.

I **didn't** play football.

3. Understanding verbs

(Verben verstehen)

Sobald die Verben gelernt sind, ist es wichtig, sie in der richtigen Weise zu verwenden, d. h. die richtige Form zu benutzen.

Zum Beispiel das Verb **(to) speak.** Es gibt viele Formen dieses Verbs: speak, speaks, spoke, spoken, speaking, don't speak, doesn't speak, have spoken etc.

Wann werden die verschiedenen Formen verwendet und warum?

(To) speak wird als Infinitiv (Grundform des Verbs) bezeichnet. Dies ist der Ausgangspunkt für alle anderen Formen des Verbs. Der Infinitiv wird für die einfache Gegenwart verwendet, um festgelegte oder regelmäßige Handlungen/Tätigkeiten und Allgemeines zu beschreiben.

Nur wenn wir über andere (dritte Person) sprechen, fügen wir dem Infinitiv ein -s oder -es hinzu. (Siehe Regeln zum -s in Point 1).

You play – he play**s** I do – he do**es**

Spoke ist die einfache Vergangenheitsform und wird für abgeschlossene Handlungen verwendet. Dies ist die einzige Form des Verbs, die für das Beschreiben beendeter Aktionen benötigt wird:

I spoke – you spoke – he spoke – she spoke – it spoke – we spoke – they spoke

Hierbei ist zu beachten, dass es sich bei **speak** um eine Verbform handelt, die eine unregelmäßige Vergangenheitsform bildet. Diese Formen können nicht durch eine Regel abgeleitet werden wie die regelmäßigen Verben (play – played), sondern müssen wie Vokabeln gelernt werden.

Spoken (die dritte Form des Verbs) wird auf viele verschiedene Arten verwendet, aber die gebräuchlichste Verwendung ist, wenn man sagen will, dass jemand irgendwann eine bestimmte Handlung ausgeführt hat. Dabei bleibt der genaue Zeitpunkt dieser Handlung unerwähnt.

(I/you/we/they **have** – he/she/it **has**)

I **have spoken** to him many times.

I **have spoken** to John about the problem.

He **has spoken** to the bank about a loan.

4. Auxiliary verbs

(Hilfsverben)

Hilfsverben sind Verben, die helfen, Sätze zu bilden und Fragen zu stellen. Das gebräuchlichste Hilfsverb ist das Verb **(to) do**. Aber es gibt auch noch andere Hilfsverben:

could, can, must, would, should, shall, will, may, might, etc.

Grundregeln

Wenn ein Hilfsverb verwendet wird, wird auch der Infinitiv des Vollverbs verwendet (die ›he/she/it, ein s muss mit‹-Regel gilt dabei nicht.)

Beispiele

I play tennis.	**He plays** tennis.	He **can play** tennis.
I bake a cake.	**He bakes** a cake.	He **can bake** a cake.
I see a specialist.	**He sees** a specialist.	He **should see** a specialist.

Wichtig – ein s wird nicht benötigt, wenn Hilfsverben verwendet werden!

Hilfsverben & Verneinungen

Wird ein Satz mit einem Hilfsverb verneint, wird nur dieses Hilfsverb verneint, nicht das Vollverb. Das Wort, das für die Verneinung von Hilfsverben verwendet wird, ist **NOT** – meistens wird es in der Kurzform verwendet.

auxiliary	**long form**	**short form**
do	do not	don't
does	does not	doesn't
can	cannot	can't
could	could not	couldn't
must	must not	mustn't
would	would not	wouldn't
should	should not	shouldn't
shall	shall not	shan't
will	will not	won't
might	might not	mightn't
may	may not	–

Beispielsätze

He **could not** eat his breakfast./He couldn't **eat** his breakfast.

Hilfsverb verneint — Vollverb im Infinitiv

Point 2 Progress test
Using the right verbs

1. Right or wrong?

Decide if these sentences are right or wrong. Correct them if necessary, as in the examples.

Stella makes a big party at Christmas.	***Wrong!*** *Stella* ***has*** *a big party at Christmas.*
Tom goes on holiday twice a year.	**Correct**
1. Can you cook some coffee to wake us up?	______________________
2. If you do a mistake, cross it out.	______________________
3. Let's make a bike trip on Sunday!	______________________
4. I took many photos on holiday.	______________________
5. He spent his bonus to Oxfam.	______________________
6. I can make business with her.	______________________
7. I get up at six o'clock.	______________________
8. Do you look a lot of television?	______________________
9. Does your wife make a lot of sport?	______________________
10. I'm listening to my new CD.	______________________

2. Do

Complete the questions using the correct form of do, as in the examples.

Where ***do*** *you come from?*

Where ***does*** *he live?*

1. ________ you live in a big city?
2. What ________ you do?
3. ________ he like his job?
4. ________ you travel a lot in your job?

5. _________ you watch the game last night?

6. _________ you work for a big company?

7. Where _________ your parents live?

8. _________ you go to Spain last week?

9. How are you _________?

10. What is that man _________?

11. Are you _________ a marathon again?

12. _________ you have any children?

13. What _________ your daughter do?

14. _________ you pick your daughter's name?

15. What _________ your wife do?

3. Verbs

Use the verbs in brackets, in the correct form to finish the sentences, as in the examples.

Yesterday I ***did*** *my English homework. (do)*

What are you ***doing****? (do)*

1. Did you _________ your homework yesterday? (do)

2. Oh no, I _________ six mistakes in my test! (make)

3. Paul is _________ a pizza. It smells great! (bake)

4. Steve _________ a French course in 1989. (do)

5. I _________ a party on Saturday. (have)

6. Paul is _________ to a party now. (go)

7. He _________ a lot of business with Japan. (do)

8. I always _________ breakfast at seven. (eat)

9. Paul _________ sport. (do)

10. Are you _________ a cake? (make)

Point 3

Ask the right questions

Dies sind die sechs wichtigsten Verben bzw. Verbformen, die man benötigt, um Fragen zu stellen:

1. Do …	4. Is/are/am + ing
2. Does …	5. Have/has
3. Did …	6. Is/are/am/was/were

1. Simple present (do)

Do wird mit **I/you/we/they** verwendet, um nach Dingen zu fragen, die feststehen, also sich nicht oft ändern:

Do you live in London? – all the time

Do you like tennis? – in general

Do your parents live near you?

2. Simple present (does – third person singular)

Does verwendet man ebenfalls für Fragen nach feststehenden Dingen, allerdings für die dritte Person Singular (he/she/it):

Does *she* live in Cologne? – all the time

Does *he* work in the city? – every day

Does *he* play football? – every week

3. Simple past (did)

Did wird für Fragen, die die Vergangenheit betreffen, verwendet, also für Fragen nach abgeschlossenen Handlungen. Hierbei ist es egal, nach welcher *Person* (I/you/he) man fragt:

Did *you* finish your book?

Did *the baby* sleep well last night?

Did *Bob* win the game?

Did *your parents* get home ok?

4. Present progressive (is/are/am)

Is/are/am sind Signalwörter für das **present progressive**. Jemand fragt, was jetzt gerade passiert, in diesem Moment, oder was zurzeit im Leben eines anderen passiert.

is – benutzt mit **he/she/it**
are – benutzt mit **you/we/they**
am – benutzt mit **I**

Is he going to the supermarket?

Is she working in the garden?

Are you doing your homework now?

Are you reading a good book at the moment?

Are we going now?

Are your parents still building their new home?

Am I annoying you?

5. Present perfect

Have/has werden mit der dritten Form (Partizip) des Verbs verwendet, um das **present perfect** zu bilden. Diese Zeit ist am schwierigsten zu lernen und zu verstehen, weil sie auf so viele verschiedene Arten verwendet werden kann und kein richtiges Äquivalent im Deutschen hat.

Einer der häufigsten Sätze in dieser Form ist die Frage **have you ever**, **has he/she ever**.

Have you ever **played** football?

Have you ever **eaten** shark meat?

Have you ever **swum** in the sea?

Have you ever **ridden** a horse?

Have you ever **broken** a leg?

Has he ever **visited** Rome?

Has she ever **eaten** sushi?

Has John ever **parachuted**?

Has Sue ever **ridden** a donkey?

Has he ever **broken** a bone?

Eine andere gebräuchliche Anwendung ist die Frage **how long ...**

How long have you **been** married?

How long have you **lived** here?

How long have you **known** Jim?

How long have you **worked** here?

6. Is/are/am/was/were (ohne ing-Form)

Beispiele

Simple present	**Simple past**
I **am** here.	I **was** here.
They **are** married.	They **were** married
We **are** very happy.	We **were** very happy
You **are** moody.	You **were** moody.
He **is** excited.	He **was** excited.
She **is** beautiful.	She **was** beautiful.
It **is** raining.	It **was** raining.

Remember:

am/is ⟶ was

are ⟶ were

Comparison (Vergleich)

Eine der besten Methoden, die verschiedenen Verbformen zu üben, besteht darin, Fragen zu stellen und deren Verwendung zu vergleichen.

Nehmen wir erneut das Verb **(to) speak** als Beispiel:

a. Simple present (all the time)

Do you speak English?	Yes, I **do**.
Do you speak English every day?	Yes, I **do**.

b. Simple present (Third person singular)

Does your wife speak English?	Yes, she **does**.
Does your wife speak English every day?	No, she **doesn't**.

c. Simple past (finished actions)

Did you **speak** English yesterday?	Yes, I **spoke** English yesterday.
Did your wife **speak** English yesterday?	Yes, she **spoke** English yesterday.

d. Present progressive (Happening right now or going on in your life at the moment)

Are you speaking to Tom?	Yes, I am.
Is he still not **speaking** to his brother?	No, he isn't.
Am I speaking too quickly for you?	Yes, you are.

e. Present perfect (Have you ever in your life?)

Have you ever **spoken** to a Russian person? Yes, **I have**.
Has your wife ever **spoken** to a Russian? Yes, **she has**.

Nicht vergessen!

Die Signalwörter müssen verwendet werden. Die meisten Fehler werden gemacht, weil die **falsche Form** gewählt wurde. Um Fragen richtig zu beantworten, achtet man immer auf die Signale: Was fragen die Leute? Was wollen Sie? Fragen sie nach Dingen, die man die ganze Zeit macht? Oder nach Dingen, die man gestern getan hat, oder was man jetzt gerade macht?

Point 3 – Progress test
Ask the right questions

1. Finish the sentences

Finish the questions using the correct verb forms.

1. ________ she still live in London?
2. ________ he work in the city?
3. ________ she play volleyball?
4. ________ she working in Spain?
5. Did you ________ English yesterday?
6. ________ you ever played squash?
7. ________ he ever visited Madrid?
8. ________ you ever eaten kangaroo?
9. Are you ________ a good book?
10. ________ we going now?
11. ________ she left?
12. ________ you ever swum in the ocean?

13. ________ you ever driven a sports car
14. ________ he going to the supermarket?
15. ________ John ever bungee jumped?
16. ________ you speak English yesterday?
17. Has Sue ever ________ a donkey?
18. ________ you ever broken a leg?
19. Has he ever ________ a bone?
20. How long have you ________ ill?
21. How long ________ you worked here?
22. How long have you ________ your wife?
23. How long ________ he worked here?
24. ________ your wife speak English?
25. ________ you speak to Syd yesterday?
26. ________ you doing your housework?
27. ________ that someone at the door?
28. Where ________ your parents live?
29. ________ Paul coming to the party?
30. ________ you spoken to him?

Point 4

Get to know your capital letters

Die korrekte Anwendung der Groß- und Kleinschreibung ist sehr wichtig für jede/n in der Wirtschaft (die/der viele E-Mails schreiben muss) und für Schülerinnen, die Tests oder Prüfungen schreiben. Bei Geschäftsleuten machen E-Mails, die mit Rechtschreibfehlern und schlechter Großschreibung übersät sind, einen sehr schlechten Eindruck. Für Schulerinnen könnte fehlerhafte Groß- und Kleinschreibung den Unterschied zwischen einer sehr guten und einer sehr schlechten Note ausmachen.

Das Verwenden von Großbuchstaben ist auf Englisch manchmal schwierig (besonders für Deutsche), weil in der deutschen Sprache Substantive groß geschrieben werden. Dies ist im Englischen nicht der Fall.

The basic rules of capitalisation in English

(Grundlegendes zur Groß- und Kleinschreibung im Englischen)

Großbuchstaben werden für folgende Dinge verwendet:

– **Proper nouns** (Eigennamen)

Proper nouns sind die Namen von Menschen, Orten, Ländern, Sprachen, Unternehmen, Wochentagen und Monaten des Jahres.

– Das Personalpronomen **I**

I (ich) wird immer groß geschrieben, egal wo es im Satz verwendet wird.

– Der Beginn eines Briefes oder einer E-Mail

Der Beginn des neuen Absatzes nach der Anrede wird – im Gegensatz zum Deutschen – immer groß geschrieben. (Dear John, **I**t was nice to see you …)

Beispiele	**I** speak **French**.	**I** work for **Johnson & Co**.
I like **Eric**.	Tom lives in **London**.	**I** play tennis on **Fridays**.
I like sport.	**I** was born in **Spain**.	My birthday is in **June**.

Alle anderen Substantive werden klein geschrieben, es sei denn, sie stehen am Anfang eines Satzes.

I play **rugby**.	Would you like **a drink**?	She wants **a car**.
He's got **a cat**.	**I**'ve got a new **computer**.	It's my **birthday**.
It's a great **hotel**.	My mother is **a nurse**.	

Point 4 – Progress test
Get to know your capital letters

1. E-mail

Find and underline all the mistakes you can find in the e-mail below, as in the example.

Dear **john**

Thank you for your E-mail. I am disappointed about yesterday's Meeting. But we have to find a Solution. I phoned alan yesterday, maybe he will spend more money on the Project. I also asked tracey to send me some Information from the london Office. I have a Meeting with tim on monday and with john at the beginning of october.

I will keep you informed about the Situation.

Best wishes
Joe

2. Right or wrong?

Decide if these sentences are right or wrong.

Correct them if necessary, as in the examples.

Put the rubbish in a Container. ***Wrong!*** *Put the rubbish in a* ***container****.*

My birthday is in March. ***Correct!***

1. Let's go to the pub tonight. ________________
2. Who paid for your tickets? ________________
3. He speaks German and Dutch. ________________
4. The holiday Inn is on East Road. ________________
5. i like beer, but i don't like wine. ________________
6. There were 20 Men in the house. ________________
7. Would you like to come to my party? ________________
8. Hamburgers are popular in America. ________________
9. Do you like my Song? ________________
10. I'm listening to the Radio. ________________

Point 5
Is it singular or plural?

Die häufigsten Fehler bei der Verwendung der Singular- und Pluralformen von Substantiven treten auf, wenn zählbare und unzählbare Substantive verwechselt werden.

Die Grundregeln

I **am** he/she/it **is** we/you/they **are**

Achtung: **is/am** wird in der Vergangenheitsform zu **was**, **are** wird zu **were**.

I/he/she/it **was** we/you/they **were**

This (diese/s/r) wird im Singular verwendet.
this person/**this** dog/**this** pencil
these (diese) ist die Pluralform.
these people/**these** dogs/**these** pencils

Dinge, die aus zwei Teilen bestehen, sind haben keine Singularform. Beispiele sind:
jeans (two legs), trousers (two legs), glasses, scissors, shorts, pyjamas, tights.

I like **these** jeans. These **shorts** are horrible.
I want **these** glasses.

Irregular words

Manche Substantive haben unregelmäßige Pluralformen, die auswendig gelernt werden müssen. Bei folgenden Wörtern ist Vorsicht geboten:

one child – two **children**	one mouse – two **mice**	one person – two **people**
one sheep – two **sheep**	one man – two **men**	one woman – two **women**
one tooth – two **teeth**	one foot – two **feet**	one goose – two **geese**

Wörter, die auf -f oder -fe enden, werden im Plural mit -ves geschrieben:

one dwarf – two **dwarves**	one wolf – two **wolves**	one loaf – two **loaves**
one knife – two **knives**	one life – two **lives**	one wife – two **wives**

Ausnahme: one belief, two **beliefs**

Der Plural von Personalpronomen:

you – your**self**	me – my**self**	her – her**self**	him – him**self**
they – them**selves**	you (plural) – your**selves**	we – our**selves**	

We are bedeutet ›wir sind‹ und kann im Gegensatz zum Deutschen nicht verwendet werden, um eine Anzahl von Menschen oder Dinge anzugeben (›Wir sind zu zehnt‹). Dafür muss **there are** benutzt werden:

There are 10 people in this room (or there are **10 of us**).

Uncountables (Unzählbares)

Wörter wie **homework** und **housework** sind nicht zählbar, daher haben sie keine Pluralform (es wird kein -s hinzugefügt). Alle diese Wörter werden ohne Artikel (a/an) verwendet.

information	–	I have **some information** for you.
advice	–	Do you need **advice**?
progress	–	We made **progress** in the negotiations yesterday.
news	–	I have **news** for you.

Dinge, die **verschiedene Formen und Größen haben** und daher schwer zu zählen sind, werden als unzählbar eingestuft: furniture, money and traffic.

Dinge, die man **nicht zählen kann**, sind natürlich unzählbar. Beispiele:

sand, meat, water, bread, coffee.

(Nicht zu verwechseln mit **einem Stück Fleisch**, **einem Stück Brot** oder **einer Tasse Kaffee – die Stücke und die Tassen sind in diesem Fall die zählbaren Dinge.**)

Dinge, die nicht gesehen werden können, werden als unzählbar eingestuft:

information, progress, advice, air, oxygen.

Spelling tips

Remember to add -**es** after -o/-ss/-x/-ch/-sh

One potato	–	two potat**oes**
One mass	–	two mass**es**
One fox	–	two fox**es**

Change **-fe** into **-ves** for plurals

one wife	–	two wi**ves**
one knife	–	two kni**ves**
one life	–	two li**ves**

Remember to use -**ies** for words ending in **consonant + y:**

family	–	famil**ies**	baby	–	bab**ies**
city	–	cit**ies**	hobby	–	hobb**ies**

Point 5 – Progress test
It is singular or plural?

1. Plurals test

Write down the plural forms of these words.

book	______________	scarf	______________	box	______________
shelf	______________	man	______________	class	______________
mouse	______________	child	______________	party	______________
family	______________	woman	______________	hobby	______________
leaf	______________	watch	______________	tooth	______________
tomato	______________	bus	______________	sheep	______________
wife	______________	fox	______________	knife	______________

2. Spot the mistake

Correct the mistakes in the following sentences.

Sentences	**Mistake(s)**
1. There was a woman in the car with two mens.	______________
2. I need a new jeans.	______________
3. David is married and has three childs.	______________
4. Do you have many friend in this town?	______________
5. I like your trouser. Where did you get it?	______________
6. This scissors are not sharp.	______________
7. Some people is always late.	______________
8. The police is looking for the criminals.	______________
9. I need my glasses, but I can't find it.	______________
10. My foots are cold.	______________

Point 6

Get to grips with adjectives & adverbs

1. Ein Adjektiv beschreibt ein Nomen näher.
2. Ein Adverb beschreibt ein Verb (wie etwas getan wird.)
3. Adverbien sind immer einer Aktivität verbunden. Irgendetwas muss passieren oder jemand muss etwas tun, um ein Adverb zu benutzen.

Beispiele

adjective	**adverb**
Paul is a **nice** person.	Paul **sings** nicely.
Paul is a **normal** person.	Paul **talks** normally.
Sue is a **nice** person.	Sue **smiled** nicely at the baby.
Sue **smells** nice.	Sue **sang** nicely at the party.

Ein Adverb wird verwendet, um eine Handlung zu beschreiben oder wie jemand etwas tut.

noun + adjective	**verb + adverb**
My mother is a **beautiful** singer.	My mother **sings beautifully**.
My dad is a **slow** driver.	My dad **drives slowly**.

Adjectives ending in -ing and -ed (Adjektive, die auf -ing und -ed enden)
Adjektive, die auf **-ing** enden, beschreiben, wie etwas ist.
Adjektve, die auf -ed enden, zeigen, was jemand denkt oder fühlt.

What is it?	**How does someone feel about it?**
(Wie/Was ist es?)	(Wie fühlt es sich an?)
Science is **interesting**.	I am **interested** in science.
The speech was **boring**.	She was really **bored**.
The match was **exciting**.	She was **excited**.

Vergleiche Adjektive mit den Endungen -ing und -ed:

boring	I'm **bored** with my job.
interesting	I'm not **interested** in football anymore.
tiring	I'm always **tired** on Fridays.
satisfying	I'm **satisfied** with your work.
depressing	This weather makes me **depressed**.

Ein Adverb verwenden, um ein Adjektiv zu beschreiben

Ein Adverb wird verwendet, um ein Verb zu beschreiben (run quickly, eat slowly etc.). Aber es wird auch verwendet, um ein Adjektiv näher zu beschreiben oder zu verbessern. Ein Adverb wird vor einem Adjektiv verwendet, um dieses stärker hervorzuheben.

Beispiele

It's cold.	How cold is it?	It's **extremely** cold.
I'm sorry.	How sorry are you?	I'm **terribly** sorry.
She was lucky.	How lucky was she?	She was **unbelievably** lucky.
The flight was cheap.	How cheap?	**Reasonably** cheap.

Rechtschreibregeln

Wenn ein Adjektiv auf -e endet, bleibt das -e vor dem -ly bestehen:

polite/polite**ly** extreme/extreme**ly** absolute/absolute**ly**

Wenn ein Adjektiv auf -le (simple, terrible etc.) endet, wird das -e entfernt und ein -y hinzugefügt, um das Adverb zu bilden.

simple/sim**ply** terrible/terri**bly** reasonable/reasona**bly**

Andere Regeln

Nach den Verben **be/get/become/seem** werden *Adjektive* verwendet:

The film **became** more and more *boring*.

Your friend **seems** *nice*.

I'm tired and I'm **getting** *hungry*.

Adjektive werden auch verwendet, um zu sagen, wie jemand/etwas aussieht, fühlt, hört, schmeckt oder riecht (bei **Verben**, die **Sinne/Gefühle** ausdrücken).

You **look** *tired.*
I **feel** *tired.*
She **sounds** *tired.*
The dinner **smells** *good.*
This milk **tastes** *strange.*
That **sounds** *great.*

Adverbien werden vor einem Partizip Perfekt (3. Verbform) verwendet (z. B. injured, organised, written).
badly written
well organised
quietly spoken

Point 6 – Progress test
Get to grips with adjectives & adverbs

1. Choose the correct word

Choose the correct adjectives to complete this text.

Next week I am going on my first business trip to Australia. I am very *exciting/excited* about it. I think it will be a *fascinating/fascinated* trip because I will meet a lot of the people I have been working with for the last few years. The plane journey is about 18 hours, which I think will be very tired/tiring. I am very *interested/interesting* in seeing the Australian way of doing business. I am a little bit *worried/worrying* about speaking English. My English isn't very good. I will be *surprising/surprised* if I understand everything at the meetings. Sometimes I find it really *frustrating/frustrated* when I speak to my Australian colleagues, because I don't understand them and they don't understand me. We all get very *frustrated/frustrating*.

The offices in Australia are *amazing/amazed*. They are situated next to a big lake, the view from the offices is wonderful. I don't think I will be *bored/boring* during my stay because I have a lot of meetings planned. But I think I will be *exhausted/exhausting* when I get back. I have spoken to the boss in Australia many times, he seems a very *amusing/amused* guy. Sometimes I am *embarrassed/embarrassing* because my English is so bad, but he doesn't get *annoyed/annoying*. Sometimes, when I think about my first meeting, I feel quite *terrified/terrifying*. But I'm sure it will be a *fulfilling/fulfilled* trip.

2. Using adverbs

Use these adjectives (in the correct form) to finish the sentences, as in the example.

bad	*incredible*	*terrible*	*bad*	*surprising*
reasonable	*pleasant*	*absolute*	*extreme*	

You spill a cup of tea on your colleague's clothes. *You say: I'm* ***terribly sorry****.*

1. Your colleague finishes a job in record time. You say: ____________________
2. The restaurant is not expensive. You say: ____________________
3. You are very, very tired. You say: ____________ exhausted!
4. You are very angry with someone. You say: ____________ displeased!
5. You win first prize in a competition. You say: ____________ surprised.

Point 7

Learn your prepositions!

List of prepositions

Eine Präposition ist ein Wort, das ein Substantiv oder Pronomen auf ein anderes Wort in einem Satz bezieht.

Beispiel: The dog sat **under** the tree.

about	above	across	after	against	along
among	around	at	before	behind	below
beneath	beside	between	by	down	during
except	for	from	in	inside	into
like	near	of	off	on	onto
out of	outside	over	past	since	through
to	toward	under	until	up	upon
with	within	without	underneath	in front of	
instead of	on top of				

Präpositionen sind ein Albtraum für jeden, der Englisch lernt, weil es so viele gibt und nicht viele Regeln. Hier sind ein paar grundlegende Richtlinien:

1. Use of the most used prepositions

(Dies sind die Präpositionen, die häufig falsch verwendet werden.)

You are **good at** something.
I'm good **at French**, he's good **at sport**.

By is used for measurements.
The kitchen is three metres **by** two metres.

You are **married to** someone.
Jules is **married to** a miner.

You travel **by** car, bus, bike, train.
»It's too far to work, let's go **by bus**.«

But you go **on foot**.
»It's only two blocks, let's go **on foot**.«

At an event
»See you **at** the party.«

Look for – search
Look for something you have lost.

Look after – babysit
Look after a baby, for example.

Look at something (short time)
Look at those birds!

Watch something (for a longer time)
I **watched** the film last night.

You do something **at an age**.
I left school **at 15**, I got my first job **at 18**.

Until (how much longer?)
I have to work **until** six.

Use **by** for deadlines.
I have to do it **by** Monday.

Use **of** for locations.
It's north **of** London.

It **depends on** something/someone.
It **depends on** the weather.

On the whole
On the whole it's a wonderful idea.

At the moment
At the moment things are going well.

Working **on** something
I'm working **on** an interesting project.

Same as John (or **like** John)
Same as John I'm going to Spain.

Interested **in** something
I'm **interested in** sport and politics

Married **to** someone
Bob is married **to** my sister.

Talk **to**
Talk **to** someone who is there.

Talk **about**
Talk **about** someone who is not there.

Listen **to**
Listen **to** a CD (for a longer time.)

Throw **to**
Throw something **to** someone to catch.

Throw **at**
Throw something **at** someone to hurt them.

By (next to)
I found it **by** (next to) a tree.

Change **into** something
I will change **into** my suit, then we can go.

Painted **by**
Painted **by** Picasso.

Go **into/in** a room
He went **into/in** the changing room.

Go **through** something (a document)
Let's **go through** the schedule one more time.

Stay **at** someone's
He's staying **at** his parents' house.

Stay **with** someone
He's staying **with** his parents.

Bitten **by** an animal
He was bitten **by** a dog.

Kind **of** someone
Thank you, that is very kind **of** you.

Put **on**/take **off**
Put **on** your coat/take **off** your shoes.

look (a word) **up**
I'll look that word **up** in the dictionary.

In the long term/**in** the long run/do it **on** your own or **by** yourself.

this, **last**, **next, every**
No preposition needed. I play golf **every** Friday.

2. A comprehensive guide to prepositions

1. **on** something
   on a table
   on the fridge

2. **in** something
   in a cup
   in a room

3. go **on/to**
   go on holiday
   go to bed
   go home

4. **of** something (not ›from‹)
   a friend **of** mine
   a member **of** the team

5. **at** a time
   at eight o'clock
   at noon

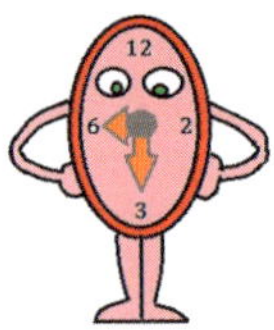

6. **on** a day or date
   on Monday
   on 1st June

7. **in** a month/year/season/
   the future
   in June
   in 1997
   in winter
   in 10 minutes

8. **at** a time of year
   at Christmas
   at Easter

9. this/last/next/every –
   no preposition
   I am playing football **this** Friday.
   I went to the cinema **last** week.
   I'm going on holiday **next** week.
   I meet John **every** Saturday.

10. **for** a period of time/
    since a point in time
    I lived there **for** 10 years.
    I have lived here **since** 1998.

11. **until** (how much longer?)
    I have to work **until** six.
    Mum is away **until** Friday.

12. **by** (a deadline)
    We have to finish **by** noon.
    We have to be there **by** 12.

13. **under** something
    The dog is **under** the table.
    The magazine is **under** the chair.

14. **between** two things
    I'm **between** jobs.
    She lives **between** two shops.

15. **behind** someone/something
    He's **behind** you.
    There's a carpark **behind**
    the café.

16. **during** (the noun)/**while**
    (the verb)
    I fell asleep **during** the film.
    I fell asleep **while** I was watching
    the film.

17. **at** the top/bottom – **in** the middle
at the top of the page
in the middle of the page
at the bottom of the page

18. **in** a vehicle/(sitting) **on** something
in a car
in a bus
in a train
on a bike.
on a horse.

19. **on** television/**on** the radio/ **on** the
Bill is **on** the telephone.
I listened to the match **on** the radio.

20. **by** car/train/bus/bike – **on** foot
I get to work **by** car.
I go to work **on** foot.
I travelled to Spain **by** train.

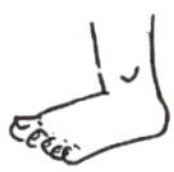

21. **at** an age
I got married **at** 23.
My son started school **at** five.

22. afraid **of** something
I'm afraid **of** spiders
Are you afraid **of** flying?

23. married **to** someone
John is married **to** a doctor.
I'm married **to** a nurse

24. good **at** something
I'm good at maths.
Are you good **at** running?

25. **from** somewhere
I'm **from** France.
My girlfriend's **from** Iceland.

3. Time prepositions

(Präpositionen der Zeit)

Die gebräuchlichsten temporalen Präpositionen sind **in**, **at**, **on**, **by**, **since** und **for**.

Manchmal ist eine Präposition nicht erforderlich. Vor allem nach **this, last, next** und **every.**

Preposit.	Use	Examples
in	a month	in July, in September
	a year	in 1985, in 1999
	seasons	in summer, in the summer of 69
	a part of the day	in the morning, in the afternoon, in the evening
	future	in a minute, in two weeks
at	part of the day	at night
	a time of day	at 6 o'clock, at midnight
	celebrations	at Christmas, at Easter
	fixed phrases	at the same time
on	days of the week	on Sunday, on Friday
	a date	on the 25. December
	special holidays	on Good Friday, on Easter Sunday, on my birthday
	a special part of a day	on the morning of 11. September
after	later than something	after school
ago	how far something happened (in the past)	six years ago
before	earlier than something	before Christmas
between	time that separates two points	between Monday and Friday
by	not later than a special time	by Thursday
during	through the whole of a period of time	during the holidays
for	a period of time	for three weeks

from … to from … until	two points form a period	from Monday to Wednesday from Monday till Wednesday from Monday until Wednesday
past	time of the day	23 minutes past six (6:23)
since	point of time	since Monday
till/until	no later than a special time	till tomorrowuntil tomorrow
to	time of the day	23 minutes to six (5:37)
up to	not more than a special time	up to six hours a day
within	during a period of time	within

4. Longer prepositions

A list of prepositions using four letters or more.

1. The picture hangs **above** my bed.
2. Our house is **opposite** the supermarket.
3. We ran **towards** the sea.
4. Death Valley is 86 metres **below** sea level.
5. Our house is **between** the supermarket and the school.
6. Our house is **beside** the supermarket.
7. We're sitting **around** the campfire.
8. They're walking **along** the beach.
9. I like being **among** people.
10. The bird flew **against** the window.
11. You mustn't go **across** this road here.
12. There isn't a bridge **across** the river.
13. **After** you!
14. You shouldn't stay **inside** the castle.
15. Can you wait **outside**?

Point 7 – Progress test
Learn your prepositions!

1. How good are your prepositions now?

Complete the sentences using the correct preposition. (Remember, sometimes no preposition is necessary!)

1. Paul is married ______ my sister.
2. They are always talking ______ me behind my back.
3. I will see you ______ next Wednesday.
4. He threw the ball ______ me and I caught it.
5. She was so angry, she threw a plate ______ me.
6. Shall we go ______ the restaurant tonight?
7. He went ______ the changing room and changed ______ his wetsuit.
8. Let's go ______ the schedule one more time.
9. This car is exactly the same ______ ours.
10. Can you look ______ my dog for two hours tonight?
11. He took ______ his coat and put ______ his shoes.
12. I am not afraid ______ snakes.
13. He rides ______ his horse.
14. She got married ______ 18.
15. Let's go ______ foot
16. He's staying ______ Bill's.
17. He is staying ______ Paula.
18. I was bitten ______ a cat.
19. That is very kind ______ you.
20. Listen ______ my new CD.

2. Time prepositions

Complete the sentences using the correct time prepositions. (Or not!!)

1. Shall we have a party ______ your birthday?
2. I'll see you ______ the party.
3. We can meet ______ next Thursday.
4. I saw Bob ______ last week.
5. I play chess ______ Sunday.
6. He fell asleep ______ the film.
7. Please deliver the goods ______ Wednesday.
8. I have to stay here ______ 12 o'clock.
9. I have been working here ______ 11 years.
10. Did you get many eggs ______ Easter?
11. I got married 13 years ______.
12. I have been working here ______ 1988.
13. Did you go to church ______ Easter Sunday?
14. Were you ______ holiday?
15. Did it snow ______ Christmas?
16. The cat always goes out ______ night.
17. Did you see your family ______ Christmas Day?
18. I had a cup of tea when I got ______ home.
19. The ambulance arrived ______ five minutes.
20. The market is on ______ Friday ______ Sunday.

Point 8
Use the apostrophe properly

Wenn wir zwei Dinge zusammenbringen, zum Beispiel einen Mann und etwas, das ihm gehört oder mit ihm verwandt ist, verwenden wir normalerweise ein Apostroph als das, **was sie zusammenfügt.**

Beispiel
My best friend is Phil. Phil has an apartment, a sister, a daughter and a fast car. If we talk about what Phil has, we would talk about:

Phil**'s** apartment
Phil**'s** sister
Phil**'s** daughter
Phil**'s** fast car

Man kann das Apostroph auch verwenden, um über Phil und das, was ihm gehört, zu sprechen, ohne das Bezugswort zu nennen:

That is **Phil's car**.
That is **Phil's**.
I went to my **sister's house**.
I went to my **sister's**.

Wenn man davon redet, irgendwohin zu gehen oder jemanden zu besuchen, spricht man von einem Ort, nicht von der Person. Zum Beispiel: **I went to my sister's** – das Apostroph bezieht sich darauf, wo sie wohnt.

Placing the apostrophe

(Platzierung des Apostrophs)

Wir verwenden ein **'s** nach einzelnen Substantiven (boy's) und Plural-Substantiven (men's), aber **s' nach Substantiven im Plural, die auf -s enden**.

These are **my parents**.
This is **their house**.
This is my **parents' house**.

Andere Beispiele

My brother**'s** bedroom (one brother)

My brother**s'** bedroom (two or more brothers)

My friend**'s** wife (one friend)

My friend**s'** wives (two or more friends, two or more wives)

The dog**'s** food (one dog)

The dog**s'** food (two or more dogs)

Tipps

Vermeide Sätze wie ›the house from Steve‹ oder ›the book of John‹. Nutze stattdessen:

Steve**'s** house

John**'s** book

Für **Menschen und Besitztümer** (Dinge, die zu ihnen gehören) benutzen wir ein Apostroph – Pete**'s** dog.

Im Beispiel

I'm at Phil'**s** (**nicht**: I'm at Phil)

bezieht sich das '**s** auf den nicht genannten **Ort** (Kurzform für: I'm at **Phil's house**), nicht auf die Person.

Point 8 – Progress test Use the apostrophe properly

1. Apostrophe Test

Re-write the sentences putting the apostrophe in correct place.

1. That womans jacket. ____________________
2. Bobs daughter. ____________________
3. My parents caravan. ____________________
4. Mens clothes. ____________________
5. A girls name. ____________________

6. A womans bicycle. ______
7. A boys school. ______
8. A birds nest. ______
9. Last nights game. ______
10. Yesterdays paper. ______
11. A years salary. ______
12. A minutes silence. ______
13. Two hours sleep. ______
14. The companys HQ. ______
15. The worlds population. ______
16. The girls club. ______
17. Hollands largest city. ______
18. A womans hat. ______
19. Next weeks meeting ______
20. A good nights sleep. ______

Point 9

Know your articles

1. A/an (unbestimmter Artikel)

Es gibt zwei allgemeine Regeln (und ihre Ausnahmen), die die Verwendung des unbestimmten Artikels **a** bzw. **an** erklären:

Regel 1 – Vokal oder Konsonant?

a + Konsonant

Beispiele:	**a** banana	**a** pear	**a** peach

an + Vokal

Beispiele:	**an** apple	**an** igloo	**an** aeroplane

Es gibt drei Ausnahmen von Regel 1:

a. Wörter, die mit **u** beginnen, aber vorne wie j ausgesprochen werden, benötigen **a**:

unit	– gesprochen junit	– daher: **a unit**
university	– gesprochen juniversity	– daher: **a university**
European	– gesprochen juropean	– daher: **a European**

b. Wörter, die mit **o** beginnen, aber vorne wie w klingen:

one	– gesprochen **wone**	– daher: **a** one-legged man
once	– gesprochen **wonce**	– daher: **a** once in a lifetime experience

c. Wörter, die mit **h** beginnen, wo das h nicht ausgesprochen wird, brauchen **an**:

honest	– gesprochen onest	– daher: he is **an** (h)onest man
		– it was **an** (h)onest mistake
honour	– gesprochen onour	– daher: it was an honour

Regel 2

Unzählbare Substantive brauchen keinen Artikel (**a or an**)

weather (we had nice weather)

furniture (we have nice furniture in our office)

information (I need information)

advice (please give me advice)

2. The (bestimmter Artikel)

Viele Wörter brauchen kein **the**, wenn man sie verallgemeinernd verwendet. Beispiele: children, music, business, industry

I like **children**.

There is a lot of **industry** in this city.

I like listening to **music**.

the wird für diese Wörter verwendet, wenn über bestimmte Dinge gesprochen wird:

the music of Mozart

the retail business (Einzelhandelsgeschäft)

Namen ohne **the**

the wird nicht mit den Namen der meisten Straßen, Parks usw. verwendet:

Park Street	Fifth Avenue	Hyde Park

the wird nicht mit den Namen von Universitäten oder Flughäfen verwendet:

JFK Airport	Cambridge University

the wird nicht verwendet, wenn das erste Wort der Name einer Person oder eines Ortes ist:

Cambridge University	Carnegie Hall

Hotels und Restaurants werden in der Regel mit **the** verwendet:

the Sheraton Hotel	**the** Bombay Restaurant

Theater, Kinos und Museen werden mit **the** verwendet:

das Nationaltheater	die Nationalgalerie	der Cinedom
the National Theatre	**the** National Gallery	**the** Cinedom

Namen mit **of** werden in der Regel mit **the** verwendet:

the Bank **of** Scotland	**the** Tower **of** London

Viele Geschäfte, Restaurants und Banken sind nach den Menschen benannt, die diese Institutionen gegründet haben, und werden ohne **the** genannt:

Lloyds Bank

Macy's

Harrods

Die Haare auf dem Kopf einer Person stehen im Singular, an anderen Stellen des Körpers ist es in der Regel Plural.

My new girlfriend has beautiful long, blonde **hair**.

I burnt the **hairs** on my arm.

Point 9 – Progress Test
Know your articles

1. The & a/an test

Choose the correct sentence

1. a. I want to study at the Cologne University.
   b. I want to study at Cologne University.

2. a. They put up a united front and won their case.
   b. They put up an united front and won their case.

3. a. We had to wait for over a hour for the bus.
   b. We had to wait for over an hour for the bus.

4. a. I saw Swan Lake at the Royal Albert Hall.
   b. I saw Swan Lake at Royal Albert Hall.

5. a. I don't believe it, she's got red hair!
   b. I don't believe it, she's got red hairs!

6. a. I don't like walking in the Hyde Park.
   b. I don't like walking in Hyde Park.

7. a. I don't like walking in the park.
   b. I don't like walking in park.

8. a. I saw a unicorn yesterday.
   b. I saw an unicorn yesterday.

9. a. There now follows an history of American culture, the programme will last approximately 16 seconds.
   b. There now follows a history of American culture, the programme will last approximately 16 seconds.

10. a. I have just seen a one-legged man.
    b. I have just seen an one-legged man

2. Choose the correct article (a or an)

1. a/an egg
2. a/an uncle
3. a/an United player
4. a/an friend
5. a/an university
6. a/an white horse
7. a/an house
8. a/an eskimo
9. a/an union
10. a/an one-man show
11. a/an hotel
12. a/an ice cream
13. a/an helmet
14. a/an hourly rate
15. a/an hope
16. a/an idiot
17. a/an acorn
18. a/an umbrella
19. a/an apple
20. a/an eagle

Point 10

Be positive about negatives

Die allgemeinen Regeln bei der Verwendung von Verneinungen lauten:

1. **don't + infinitive** benutzt man mit I/you/they/we, um über Dinge zu sprechen, die immer (nie) getan wird. **(simple present)**

I **don't play** football.

My parents **don't like** dogs.

2. **doesn't + infinitive** wird verwendet, wenn über eine andere Person oder Sache gesprochen wird **(he/she/it)**.

He **doesn't like** tennis.

She **doesn't like** football. (Never use ›he/she don't‹!!)

3. **didn't + infinitive** wird mit allen Personen verwendet, um abgeschlossene Aktionen in der Vergangenheit zu beschreiben. (**simple past**)

He **didn't come** yesterday.

I **didn't work** last week.

They **didn't go** on holiday.

4. **not + ing-Form** des Verbs wird verwendet, um zu beschreiben, was jetzt im Moment geschieht (oder nicht!). **(present progressive**)

I **am not having** breakfast.

I **am not reading** a great book at the moment.

5. **Can/can't**

Die Verneinung von **can** lautet **cannot** (oder **can't**).

I **can** swim	I **cannot** swim	I **can't** swim (Kurzform)
he **can** speak French	he **cannot** speak French	he **can't** speak French

Things to remember

– **Remember – he don't** and **don't can DO NOT EXIST!!**

– Use **doesn't** for **one** other person.

– Use **don't** for **yourself** and **more** than one other person.

– Use **didn't** for all things in the past that are finished.

Point 10 – Progress test
Be positive about negatives

1. Weekend shopping

Fill in the correct negative to finish the text.

I ________ like shopping. But every Saturday I go into town with my mother to do the weekly grocery shop. She ________ like shopping. It __________ take long to drive into town, about 10 minutes. I ________ like parking in the big, multi-storey carpark, so we leave my car in one of the side streets, the parking is cheaper there too.

I __________ stand the crowds in the market and in the stores, but it ___________ seem to bother my mother. Last week we ___________ go shopping together because my mother was ill. She __________ like missing out on our weekly get-together.

Next weekend, we are _______ going shopping because my mother is going on a trip with her friends. I am ________ going shopping on my own, so I can enjoy a nice, relaxing morning at home.

2. Choose the correct negative

Choose the correct negative to complete the sentences.

1. I like meat, but I don't like/likes fish.
2. My dad eats fish, but he don't/doesn't eat chicken.
3. I am not/don't watching the news.
4. My parents don't/doesn't listen to the radio.
5. I don't/haven't finished my homework yet.
6. Paul hasn't/haven't woken up yet.
7. I didn't/wasn't early for work today.
8. She don't/doesn't listen to a word I say.
9. My maths teacher don't/doesn't give homework at the weekend.
10. We are not/don't saving money for a house.

Point 11

Don’t confuse your words

Viele Fehler werden gemacht, wenn man entweder das falsche Wort benutzt oder ein Wort mit einem anderen verwechselt. (Oft, wenn das Wort auf Deutsch ähnlich ist.)

Hier ist eine umfassende Liste der verwirrendsten Wörter und eine Erklärung des Unterschieds zwischen den beiden Wörtern.

English	**German**	**Example sentences**
1. current/ actual	derzeitig/ tatsächlich	Who is your **current** boss? Who is your **actual** boss?
2. hardly/ hard	kaum/ hart	I **hardly** know him. I work **hard**.
3. lend/ borrow	verleihen/ borgen	Can you **lend** me some money? I need to **borrow** some money.
4. Life/ live	das Leben/ leben	**Life** is great. I **live** in Germany.
5. say/ tell	sagen/ erzählen	**Say** something. **Tell** someone something.
6. effect/ affect	Affekt/ Wirkung	She has a strange **effect** on me. How does this **affect** your job?
7. journey/ travel	eine Reise/ reisen	How was your **journey**? I like to **travel** light.
8. control/ check	steuern/ kontrollieren	Can you **control** that jeep? They **checked** the passports twice.
9. recipe/ prescription	Kochrezept/ Rezept	Have you got a **recipe** for lasagna? Did you get the **prescription** for the pills?
10. appointment/ date	Termin/ Verabredung	I made an **appointment** with the dentist. I’ve got a **date** with Jim tonight.
11. desert/ dessert	Wüste/ Dessert	The Gobi **Desert** is huge. We have strawberries for **dessert**.

12. past/ passed	Vergangenheit/ bestanden	That's all in the **past**. I **passed** my driving test.
13. advice/ advise	Beratung/ beraten	I don't need your **advice**. I would **advise** you not to do that.
14. sensible/ sensitive	sensibel/ empfindlich	She is a **sensible**, well-behaved girl. She cries a lot, she is very **sensitive**.
15. personal/ personnel	persönlich/ Personal	That is a **personal** matter. The **personnel** are getting a bonus soon.
16. lose/ loose	verlieren/ locker	Did you **lose** again? My tooth is **loose**.
17. donate/ spend	spenden/ ausgeben	I **donate** a lot of money to charity. I **spend** a lot of money on clothes.
18. accept/ except	akzeptieren/ außer	I do not **accept** your apology. Everyone came **except** Pete.
19. ready/ finished	bereit/ fertig	I'm **ready**, let's go! I've **finished**!
20. there/ their	dort/ Ihr	Put the boy over **there**. I think that is **their** car.
21. patience/ patients	Geduld/ Patienten	I am losing my **patience** with you. There were 20 **patients** at the doctor's.
22 weather/ whether	das Wetter/ ob	The **weather** is terrible today. John does not know **whether** he's coming.
23. brakes/ breaks	Bremsen/ Pausen	The **brakes** on my car are faulty. We took two coffee **breaks** today.
24. shortly/ briefly	demnächst/ kurz	Sue will be arriving **shortly**. He spoke **briefly** about his trip.
25. take/ bring	nehmen/ bringen	Can you **take** me to the airport? Can you **bring** me a coffee?
26. homework/ housework	Hausaufgaben/ Hausarbeit	Have you done your maths **homework**? I hate doing **housework**.
27. takeover/ overtake	Übernahme/ überholen	The company is planning a **takeover**. I don't like **overtaking** cars.
28. stranger/ foreigner	Fremder/ Ausländer	Don't talk to **strangers**. There are many **foreigners** here.

29. watch/ clock	Armbanduhr/ Wanduhr	I like your new **watch**. There is a big **clock** on the wall.
30. true/ the truth	wahr/ die Wahrheit	That's not **true**. Please tell me **the truth**.
31. remind/ remember	jemanden erinnern/ sich erinnern	**Remind** me to post that letter. I **remembered** your birthday!
32. It's/ its	es ist/ sein	**It's** time to leave. A good dog knows **its** place.
33. a ticket/ a card	Eine Eintritts-karte/eine Karte (Post)	I've got **a ticket** for the concert. Did you send John a birthday **card**?
34. quite/ quiet	ziemlich/ ruhig	The ring is **quite** expensive. It's very **quiet** in the woods.
35. you're/ your	Du bist/ dein	**You're** in my way. **Your** taxi is here.
36. bare/ bear	nackt/ Bär	I like walking around **bare**foot. Have you ever seen a polar **bear**?
37. cue/ queue	Cue/ Schlange	I have just bought a new snooker **cue**. There is a massive **queue** outside.
38. draught/ draft	Durchzug/ Entwurf	Close the window, there's a **draught**. This is the final **draft** of the plans.
39. principle/ principal	Prinzip/ Schuldirektor	It's not the money, it's the **principle**. Go to the school **principal**.
40. sight/ site	Sicht/ Baustelle	What a beautiful **sight**. Bob works on a building **site**.
41. story/ storey	Geschichte/ Stockwerk	Grandma loves telling fairy **stories**. It's a 10-**storey** building.
42. meter/ metre	Zähler/ Meter	There's a water **meter** in the apartment. My new flat is 60 square **metres**.
43. currents/ currants	Strömungen/ Johannis-beeren	There are strong **currents** in the water. Are you putting **currants** in the cake mix?
44. kerb/ curb	Randstein/ etw. bremsen	Don't park too near the **kerb**! He is trying to **curb** his drinking.
45. council/ counsel	Stadtrat/ jdn. beraten	The city **council** are useless. I think she needs **counselling**.

46. compliment/ complement	Kompliment/ Ergänzen	Thank you for the **compliment**. This wine **complements** the fish perfectly.
47. course/ coarse	Kurs/ vulgär	Are you still doing your French **course**? He is extremely **coarse**, I don't like him.
48. bizarre/ bazaar	seltsam/ Basar	He talks to himself, he's **bizarre**. Did you visit the grand **bazaar** in Istanbul?
49. stationary/ stationery	stationär/ Bürobedarf	He drove into the back of a **stationary** car. Do we need any office **stationery**?
50. confident/ confidential	selbstsicher/ vertraulich	He is a very **confident** person. That information is **confidential**.
51. rebate/ discount	Rückzahlung/ Preisnachlass	I got a tax **rebate**. I got a 10% **discount** on my new car.
52. back/ backside	Rücken/ Hintern	Jill's **hurt** her back. I slipped and fell on my **backside**.
53. aloud/ allowed.	laut/ erlaubt	I am always thinking **aloud**. I don't think you are **allowed** to do that!
54. cereal/ serial	Getreide/ Fernsehserie	I always have **cereal** for breakfast. Are you following the new **serial** on TV?
55. shade/ shadow	Schatten/ Schlagschatten	It's hot, let's sit in the **shade**! The tower cast a long **shadow** over the beach.
56. whose/ who's	dessen/ wer ist …	**Whose** bag is that? **Who's** taking you to the airport?
57. excess/ access	Exzess/ Zugriff	There is an **excess** charge of €50. I can't **access** my computer.
58. notice/ note	merken/ Zettel	Did he **notice** you? I've left a **note** for the milkman.
59. live/ live (2)	leben/ live	I **live** in Cologne. I love watching **live** bands.
60. alter/ altar	ändern/ Altar	Can you **alter** my jeans for me? The church has a beautiful **altar**.

Point 11 – Progress test
Confusing words

1. Confusing words

Choose the correct word to finish these sentences

1. I picked up my recipe/prescription.
2. My plane was cancelled/delayed by an hour.
3. Never lend/borrow money from a friend.
4. We always control/check each delivery.
5. Paul will be arriving shortly/briefly.
6. You really shouldn't read confident/confidential documents.
7. I sometimes talk aloud/allowed.
8. He was bare/bear when he opened the door.
9. It's/its time to go.
10. You're very quite/quiet? Is something bothering you?
11. We had to cue/queue for ages.
12. I hardly/hard know Bob.
13. Tom works hard/hardly.
14. It's on the fifth story/storey.
15. He past/passed the test.

16 I am going to see the principle/principal.

17. He works on a building sight/site.
18. There is a terrible draught/draft in here.
19. They fitted a water meter/metre in our kitchen.
20. An alter/altar is part of a church.
21. The breaks/brakes on my car don't work.
22. I usually have cereal/serial for breakfast.
23. I don't like him, he's rather course/coarse.
24. Ask Bob, he'll lend/borrow you some money.
25. I made an appointment/date with the doctor.
26. Are you putting currents/currants in that cake?
27. She broke her ankle, she fell over the kerb/curb.
28. A specialist has agreed to council/counsel her.
29. Paul complimented/complemented me.
30. Did you lose/loose the game?

Point 12

Avoid Denglish (Get to know your false friends)

Was ist ein falscher Freund?

Ein Wort, das oft mit einem Wort in einer anderen Sprache (mit einer anderen Bedeutung) verwechselt wird, weil die beiden Wörter ähnlich aussehen oder ähnlich klingen.

False friend (German)	Wrong translation (English)	Correct word	Correct use
aktuell	actual	current	What is your **current** situation?
bekommen	become	get	Did you **get** your new car?

False friend (German)	Wrong translation (English)	Correct word	Correct use
Art	art	type/sort	What **type** of person are you?
Bad	bad	bath	I think you need a **bath**!
bald	soon	bald	My granddad is **bald**.
Chef	boss	cook	Compliments to the **cook**.

Dose	dose	can/tin	Would you like a **can** of beer?
Fabrik	fabric	factory	Bob works in a **factory**.
fast	almost	fast	My new car is really **fast**.
Flur	floor	corridor	There is a machine in the **corridor**.
Gift	gift (present)	poison	I brought you a little **gift**.

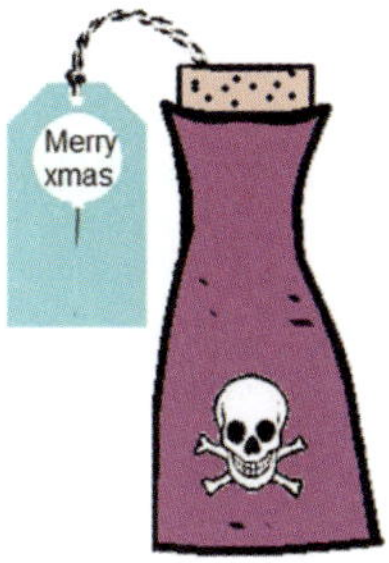

Handy	mobile phone	practical	It's **handy** having shops nearby.
Hut	hut	hat	Do you like my new **hat**?

Küche	kitchen	cuisine/food	I love Italian cuisine.
Kritik	critic	criticism	He can't take **criticism**.

Lack	varnish/finish	lack	We have a **lack** of manpower.
Mist	dung/crap	mist/fog	It's very **foggy** today.
Net	sympathetic	nice	He's a really **nice** guy.
Objektiv	lens	objective	What is your **objective**?
Personell	personal	personnel	All the **personnel** got a bonus.
prüfen	proof	check	Did you **check** the departure time?
Rat	advice	rat	There's a **rat** in the cellar.

Raten (zahlen)	rates	instalments	Can we pay in monthly **instalments**?
Reise	travel	trip	How was your **trip** to Paris?
Rezept	recipe	prescription	The doctor gave me a **prescription**.
Roman	Roman	novel	It's a wonderful **novel** by Dickens.
senden	send	broadcast	It was a live **broadcast**.
sensibil	sensible	sensitive	He's very **sensitive**, be careful.
spenden	spend	donate	I **donated** €50 to Oxfam.
weit	wide	far	It's too **far** to walk.
Dessert	Wüste	dessert	It was a lovely **dessert**.

Point 12 – Progress test
Avoid Denglish (Get to know your false friends)

1. False friends

Can you spot the false friend? Write the correct word on the right.

1. I don't like his art. ______________
2. I became a new bicycle for Christmas. ______________
3. My new chef is not very nice. ______________
4. Who is your actual girlfriend? ______________
5. I made a lot of failures in my exams. ______________
6. My new handy has got a camera. ______________
7. He is easily offended, he is very sensible. ______________
8. They put a label on the backside. ______________
9. The English kitchen isn't very good. ______________
10. They got lost in the dessert and died after five days. ______________
11. I bought a new objective for my camera. ______________
12. Always proof your car tyres before a long journey. ______________
13. RTL sent a great programme about birds last night. ______________
14. Everyone likes him, he's such a sympathetic guy. ______________
15. The hotel is too wide to walk, take a taxi. ______________
16. I do not need your rat. ______________
17. Our travel to Kenya was fascinating. ______________
18. We have a shortage of personal. ______________
19. I spent €50 to Oxfam. ______________
20. Sally works in a fabric. ______________

Point 13
Widen your vocabulary

Eine gute Möglichkeit, seinen Wortschatz zu erweitern und zu verbessern, ist das Erlernen der unterschiedlichen Bedeutung von Wörtern. Viele Wörter haben zwei oder mehr Bedeutungen. Die richtige Verwendung dieser Wörter führt rasch zu viel besserem Englisch.

1. One word – two meanings

(Ein Wort – zwei Bedeutungen)

Im Folgenden eine umfassende Liste von Wörtern mit mindestens zwei Bedeutungen. Das Erlernen dieser Wörter kann das Niveau des eigenen Englisch stark erhöhen.

English	German	How to use the words
1. (to) join	verbinden eintreten	**Join** the two pieces together with glue. Sally and I have **joined** a fitness club.
2. (to) order	bestellen befehlen	I've **ordered** the meat for Christmas. He was **ordered** to sit down by the judge.
3. environment	Umgebung Umwelt	We live in a nice **environment**. Do you care about the **environment**?
4. own	besitzen eigen	I **own** an old Bentley Do you have your **own** house?
5. change	Wechselgeld Änderung	Do you have any small **change**? We had to **change** the locks on the door.
6. (to) avoid	jmdn. meiden vermeiden	I **avoid** talking to him. We try to **avoid** overspending at Christmas.
7. safe	sicher Tresor	Is that bridge **safe**? But your belongings in the **safe**.
8. (to) save	retten sparen	He was **saved** by the coastguard. I am trying to **save** money.
9. cook	kochen Koch	What are you **cook**ing? He is a great **cook**.

10. (to) manage	leiten hinkriegen	He **manages** the department very well. We **managed** to solve the problem.
11. slip	Zettel rutschen	Write your number down on a **slip** of paper. He **slipped** on the ice, but he's OK.
12. bottle	Flasche Mut	But the empty **bottle** in the kitchen. He hasn't got the **bottle** to jump.
13. state	Staatlich Zustand	My mother gets a **state** pension. Your car is in a terrible **state**.
14. (to) skip	auslassen hüpfen	Let's **skip** lunch and go to dinner this evening. The girls are **skipping** in the garden.
15. (to) strike	schlagen streiken	Did he **strike** you? The workers have gone on **strike** for more money.
16. (to) settle	ansiedeln abklären	They have **settled** in New Zealand. We **settled** the dispute eventually.
17. space	Platz Weltraum	Do you have enough **space** in your garage? I would love to travel in **space**.
18. reason	Grund argumentieren	What was the **reason** for the argument? You cannot r**eason** with him, he's impossible!
19. play	spielen Theaterstück	Ron is **playing** with the children in the garden. Did you enjoy the **play** last night?
20. rare	selten blutig	White lions are very **rare**. I would like my streak **rare**.
21. value	Wert schätzen	What is the **value** of your house now? I really **value** my friends.
22. (to) try	vor Gericht stellen versuchen	He was **tried** in the high court for his crimes. I **try** to lose weight, but it doesn't work.
23. foil	Verhindern Folie	The kidnap plot was **foiled** by the police Wrap the chicken in **foil** and put it in the oven.
24. yellow	Gelb feige	Why did you paint your garage **yellow**? He ran away because he was **yellow**.

25. cross	Böse Kreuz	My mother is very **cross** with you. I like your silver **cross**, where did you buy it?
26. (to) cry	schreien weinen	He **cried** for mercy. She **cried** when she got the terrible news.
27. water	gießen Wasser	Could you **water** my plants while I'm away? Would you like a glass of **water**?
28. patient	geduldig Patient	He is very **patient** with his pupils. My doctor treats his **patients** very well.
29. plant	Pflanze Werk	Do you have any **plants** in your office? Sue works in a chemical **plant**.
30. kid	Kind jdn. veräppeln	He's a nice **kid**. Are you **kidding** me?
31. dart	Pfeil flitzen	They used poisoned **darts** to kill the spy. He was **darting** from one place to the other.
32. minute	Minute winzig	I'll be with you in one **minute**. The particles are **minute**.
33. (to) cut	schneiden absenken	**Cut** the cake into eight pieces. We are trying to **cut** costs.
34. view	Meinung Ausblick	What is your **view** of the situation? We had a lovely **view** from our hotel window.
35. class	Klasse Rang	I'm in the 4th **class** now. They are a third **class** team.
36. like	mögen wie	I **like** going to the theatre. You look **like** Brad Pitt.
37. true	wahr treu	Is what you are saying **true**? She stayed **true** to him throughout the separation.
38. match	Spiel Streichholz	Did you see the **match**? Do you have a **match**?
39. force	zwingen Kraft	He was **forced** to leave the company. My new car has a lot of **force**.
40. tip	Trinkgeld tippen	I usually leave a **tip** if I am happy with the service. I **tipped** them to win and they did.

41. dress	Kleid anziehen	I like your new **dress**. Get **dressed**, we have to go.
42. bear	ertragen Bär	I can't **bear** this music. Did you see the polar **bears** at the zoo?
43. (to) charge	berechnen angreifen	They **charged** me €20 for delivery. The police **charged** the demonstrators.
44. nurse	wiegen Kranken-schwester	He **nursed** the baby in his arms. My sister is a **nurse**.
45. term	Ausdruck Semester	What is the **term** for people who are out of work? I will have to work harder next **term**.
46. draw	Unentschieden zeichnen	We scored first, but it ended in a **draw**. I can't **draw** very well.
47. stamp	Briefmarke I was younger. stampfen	I used to collect **stamps** when The crowd were **stamping** their feet.
48. key	Tonart Schlüssel	What **key** do you sing that song in? Who's got the **key** to the door?
49. express	ausdrücken Schnellzug	He can't **express** himself at all. We took the **express** to the airport.
50. mass	Gottesdienst Menge	I attended midnight **mass** at Christmas. There were a **mass** of people in the airport.
51. log	Holzklotz registrieren	Put another **log** on the fire. You have to **log** in first.
52. sound	solide Geräusch	That is a very **sound** idea. What was that **sound**?
53. iron	bügeln eisern	Could you **iron** my short for me? Is that made out of **iron**?
54. part	trennen Teil	They've **parted** company. It's all **part** of the job.
55. count	Graf zählen	**Count** Dracula is really scary. Tommy can **count** to 20 now.
56. catch	fangen Haken	**Catch** the ball and throw it back. That's very cheap, what's the **catch**?

57. fringe	Pony Rand	You look pretty with a **fringe**. He is always on the **fringe**, he never gets involved.
58. break	brechen Pause	Did you **break** that vase? We need to take a **break**.
59. palm	Handfläche Palme	Rub the cream into the **palm** of your hands. I love **palm** trees on the beach.
60. hand	Hand Applaus	It's in your right **hand**. That was great, give him a big **hand**!

2. Words that look the same – but sound different

(Wörter, die gleich aussehen – aber anders klingen)

Viele Wörter werden gleich geschrieben, haben aber unterschiedliche Bedeutungen und Aussprachen. Diese Tabelle und die Erklärungen können helfen, zwischen den verschieden klingenden Wörtern zu unterscheiden.

English words	**German words**	**Pronunciation (Phonetics)**	**Example sentences**
1. row	rudern Reihe streiten	rəu rəu rau	We are **rowing** across the water. Plant the seeds in a **row**. Mum and dad had a big **row**.
2. read	lesen las	ri:d red	Do you like **read**ing books? I **read** the news last night.
3. close	nah schließen schwül	kləus kləuz kləus	I was very **close** to my mother. Please **close** the window. It is very **close** in here.
4. house	Haus unterbringen	haus haʊz	Welcome to my **house**. That building can **house** 10 families.
5. use	benutzen Nutzung	ju:z ju:s	Please **use** the lift. What **use** is that?
6. wind	Wind wickeln	wɪnd waɪnd	The **wind** is blowing hard. **Wind** the bandage around your foot.
7. tear	Träne zerreißen	tɪər tɛər	He eyes were full of **tears**. Don't **tear** my shirt.

8. lead	leiten Blei	liːd led	He **leads** the pack. That contains **lead**.
9. P(p)olish	Polnisch Putzmittel	ˈpoʊ.lɪʃ ˈpɑː.lɪʃ	Ivan is **Polish**. Where's the shoe **polish**?
10. wound	gewickelt Wunde	waʊnd wuːnd	He **wound** the wire around the pan. That's a very nasty **wound** you have.
11. present	Geschenk Gegenwart präsentieren	ˈprez.ənt ˈprez.ənt prɪˈzent	That's a nice **present**. I live for the **present**. I have to **present** it tomorrow.
12. bow	sich verbeugen Schleife	baʊ boʊ	Take a **bow**! She wrapped a **bow** around the gift.

3. Words that sound the same but are written differently (and have different meanings)

Viele Wörter klingen gleich oder ähnlich, werden aber anders geschrieben und haben unterschiedliche Bedeutungen.

English	**German**
altar/alter	*Altar/ändern*
bazaar/bizarre	*Basar/Bizarr*
brake/break	*Bremse/Pause*
cereal/serial	*Getreide/Serie*
chord/cord	*Akkord/Schnur*
current/currant	*aktuelle/Johannisbeere*
dual/duel	*zweifach/Zweikampf*
pole/poll	*Pole/Umfrage*
coarse/course	*grob/Kurs*
queue/cue	*Warteschlange/Billardstock*
aloud/allowed	*laut/erlaubt*

Point 13 – Progress test
Widen your vocabulary

1. One word – two meanings

*Choose the German word that matches the English word in **bold**, as in the example.*

***Wind** the bandage around the wound.*	*Wind/**wickeln***
1. The game ended in a **draw.**	unentschieden/zeichnen
2. Can you **iron** my shirt, please?	bügeln/eisern
3. I am trying hard to **save** money.	retten/sparen
4. Are you going to midnight **mass**?	Gottesdienst/Menge
5. I wrote my number on a **slip** of paper.	Zettel/rutschen
6. Did you **join** the fitness club?	verbinden/eintreten
7. They offer third-**class** service.	Klasse/Rang
8. Have you got the **key** to the caravan?	Tonart/Schlüssel
9. Did you **log** on?	Holzklotz/registrieren
10. When did you **break** that vase?	brechen/Pause

2. Words that sound the same but are written differently

Choose the correct word to fix the description.

1. A line of people or vehicles.	cue/queue
2. A breakfast food made from grains.	serial/cereal
3. Having two parts.	dual/duel
4. Happening now.	current/currant
5. A Middle Eastern market.	bizarre/bazaar
6. A group of musical notes.	chord/cord
7. A long, slender piece of wood.	Pole/pole
8. To stop a vehicle.	break/brake
9. Rough.	coarse/course
10. A sacred table in a church.	alter/altar

Point 14

Get to know your silent letters

Stumme Buchstaben (silent letters) sind Buchstaben, die nicht zu hören sind, wenn das Wort gesprochen wird, aber gesehen werden können. Es gibt keine allgemeine Regel. Sie müssen gelernt werden.

Das Beherrschen von **silent letters** verbessert die Aussprache erheblich und der nächste Abschnitt erklärt warum.

Sprich die folgenden Wörter laut aus:

bomb would climber almond salmon sword

Alle diese Wörter enthalten stumme Buchstaben. Wenn diese Buchstaben ausgesprochen werden, ist es falsch!

bom**b** wou**l**d clim**b**er a**l**mond sa**l**mon s**w**ord

Alle rot markierten Buchstaben sind stumm und werden nicht verwendet, wenn das Wort ausgesprochen wird:

almond ist zum Beispiel ›amond‹ – stummes l, **salmon** ist ›samon‹ – stummes l, und **sword** ist ›sord‹ – stummes w.

Dies ist eine Liste der beliebtesten Wörter mit stummen Buchstaben und einem Ausspracheführer.

Die Sätze sollten geübt werden, wobei darauf zu achten ist, dass die Wörter mit Buchstaben, die in Rot hervorgehoben sind, richtig ausgesprochen werden.

Silent letters	**Pronunciation (Phonetics)**	**Example sentences**
Silent b		
lam**b**	læm	I love lamb.
thum**b**	θʌm	John hurt his thumb yesterday.
num**b**	nʌm	My feet are numb.
crum**b**	krʌm	Don't drop crumbs on the floor.
clim**b**ing	ˈklaɪmɪŋ	Are you going climbing tomorrow?
bom**b**	bɒm	There's a bomb in the city.

com**b**	kəʊm	Comb your hair, you look a mess.
dou**b**t	daʊt	I have no doubt you'll make it.
plum**b**er	ˈplʌmə(r)	The sink is leaking, we need a plumber.
lim**b**	lɪm	I will tear him limb from limb!
de**b**t	det	Ronnie is in a lot of debt.
tom**b**	tuːm	They found the mummy in a forgotten tomb.
Silent d		
e**d**ge	ege	That table has got sharp edges.
he**d**ge	edʒ	Dad is cutting the hedge.
We**d**nesday	ˈwenzdeɪ	It's my birthday on Wednesday.
han**d**some	ˈhæns(ə)m	Paul is so handsome.
han**d**kerchief	ˈhæŋkə(r)ˌtʃɪf	I can't find my handkerchief.
ba**d**ge	bædʒ	That's a nice badge?
we**d**ge	wedʒ	Put a wedge in the door.
Silent g		
gnome	nəʊm	I hate garden gnomes.
si**g**n	saɪn	What does that sign mean?
resi**g**n	rɪˈzaɪn	The trainer has resigned.
desi**g**n	ɪˈzaɪn	What a great design!
forei**g**ner	ˈfɒrɪnə(r)	He is a foreigner?
Silent h		
w**h**at	wɒt	What did you say?
w**h**en	wen	When is Yvonne coming?
w**h**y	waɪ	Why are you looking at me?
w**h**ich	wɪtʃ	Which house is yours?
g**h**ost	gəʊst	There's a ghost in my house.
honest	ˈɒnɪst	He is not being very honest.
hour	ˈaʊə(r)	I'll be home in one hour.
w**h**ite	waɪt	My car is white.
r**h**ythm	ˈrɪðəm	That's a nice rhythm.
Silent k		
knife	naɪf	Please pass me the knife.

knee	niː	I hurt my knee.
knot	nɒt	Tie a knot in that rope.
knitting	ˈnɪtɪŋ	Are you good at knitting?
know	nəʊ	Do you know Bob?
knob	nɒb	Press the green knob to start the machine.
knock	nɒk	Was that a knock on the door?
knickers	ˈnɪkə(r)z	She was wearing blue knickers.
knuckle	ˈnʌk(ə)l	He hurt his knuckles on the stone.
knight	naɪt	A knight in shining armour.
knew	njuː	I knew him at school.
Silent l		
a**l**mond	ˈɑːmənd	This cake has got almonds in it.
pa**l**m	pɑːm	I love palm trees.
yo**l**k	jəʊk	Egg yolks are yellow.
sa**l**mon	ˈsæmən	Would you like some fresh salmon?
ca**l**f	kɑːf	Look at the young calf!
ha**l**f	hɑːf	Would you like half an orange?
cha**l**k	tʃɔːk	Where is my piece of chalk?
ta**l**k	tɔːk	Did you talk to him at the party?
wa**l**k	wɔːk	Shall we go for a walk?
fo**l**k	fəʊk	They are peaceful folk.
wou**l**d	wʊd	I would like to make a complaint.
shou**l**d	ʃʊd	You should ask before you take things.
cou**l**d	kʊd	Could I use your telephone, please?
Silent n		
autum**n**	ˈɔːtəm	I love the trees in autumn.
dam**n**	dæm	Where is that damn bus?
hym**n**	hɪm	What is your favourite hyme?
colum**n**	ˈkɒləm	The motorway is supported by huge columns.
Silent p		
recei**p**t	rɪˈsiːt	Did you get a receipt for the computer?
psychology	saɪˈkɒlədʒi	Harry is studying psychology
pneumonia	njuːˈməʊniə	Mum has got pneumonia.

Silent s		
i**s**land	ˈaɪlənd	I would love to live on a tropical island.
i**s**le	aɪl	Have you ever visited the Isle of Man?
ai**s**le	aɪl	I would like an aisle seat on the plane.
Silent t		
wi**t**ch	wɪtʃ	The wicked witch of the west.
fas**t**en	ˈfɑːs(ə)n	Fasten your coat before you go out.
cas**t**le	ˈkɑːs(ə)l	That is a beautiful castle.
wa**t**ch	wɒtʃ	That's a big watch!
lis**t**en	ˈlɪs(ə)n	Please listen to what I say.
chris**t**mas	ˈkrɪsməs	I'll see you at Christmas.
mor**t**gage	ˈmɔː(r)gɪdʒ	We can't afford a mortgage.
sof**t**en	ˈsɒf(ə)n	I will try to soften the butter.
of**t**en	ˈɒf(ə)n	How often do you go on holiday?
Silent u		
g**u**est	gest	He is our guest of honour.
g**u**ess	ges	Try to guess my age.
g**u**itar	gɪˈtɑː(r)	Can you play guitar?
g**u**ard	gɑː(r)d	There is a guard at every entrance.
b**u**ilding	ˈbɪldɪŋ	Which building do you work in?
g**u**ilty	ˈgɪlti	He was found guilty.
rog**ue**	rəʊg	He is such a rogue.
vog**ue**	vəʊg	Fake news is very much in vogue.
bisc**u**it	ˈbɪskɪt	Would you like a chocolate biscuit?
tong**ue**	tʌŋ	Hold your tongue!
Silent w		
ans**w**er	ˈɑːnsə(r)	Did you get an answer from Tracy?
wren	ren	I saw a little wren in the garden.
write	raɪt	I wrote 15 postcards when I was in Spain.
wrestling	ˈres(ə)lɪŋ	Do you like wrestling?
wriggle	ˈrɪg(ə)l	Stop wriggling!
wrinkle	ˈrɪŋk(ə)l	Tom has a lot of wrinkles on his face.
s**w**ord	sɔː(r)d	That is a beautiful ornamental sword.

whole	həʊl	I promise to tell the whole truth.
wreck	rek	They found the wreck on the seabed.
t**w**o	tuː	Two coffees, please!
wrap	ræp	Can you wrap that for me, please?
wrong	rɒŋ	That is the wrong answer.
wrist	rɪst	I have broken my wrist.
write	raɪt	Did he write to you?

Point 14 – Progress test
Get to know your silent letters

1. Odd man out

Three of the words have silent letters, one doesn't. Which is the ***odd man out****, write your answer on the right.*

				answer
1. climb	comb	doubt	elbow	______
2. hour	exhaust	exhibition	inhale	______
3. column	hymn	autumn	hyphen	______
4. kill	know	knot	knife	______
5. swords	answer	swing	write	______
6. wade	handsome	Wednesday	grandson	______
7. guest	guilt	tongue	language	______
8. island	grasp	isle	Illinois	______
9. receipt	psychology	pneumonia	petal	______
10. whole	salmon	half	calm	______
11. welcome	write	wren	two	______
12. fasten	listen	castle	taste	______
13. biscuit	under	tongue	guard	______
14. sing	sign	design	foreigner	______
15. would	should	colour	could	______

Point 15

Understand the will future

Viele Leute machen Fehler, wenn sie Englisch sprechen, weil sie die falsche Zeit benutzen. Ein perfektes Beispiel dafür ist der falsche Gebrauch des **will future**, wenn über zukünftige feste Pläne gesprochen wird.

1. Present progressive für zukünftige feste Pläne

Wenn es um **zukünftige feste Pläne** geht, wird das **progressive** (ing-Form) benutzt.

Die ing-Form wird für gerade stattfindende (temporäre) Situationen verwendet. Temporäre Situationen in der Vergangenheit, in der Gegenwart und in der Zukunft.

Beispiele

past

This time yesterday I was driving to Bonn.

present

I am driving to Bonn. **(happening in your life at the moment)**

I am reading a good book.

future

I am driving to Bonn tonight.

Wenn man über Dinge spricht, die in der Zukunft oder für eine vorübergehende Zeit getan werden (einen Film ansehen, in einem Hotel bleiben, ein Spiel spielen), braucht man das **present progressive with a future meaning**.

A future time	is/are/am	-ing form of the verb
Next week	*my mother is*	*visiting us*
On Sunday	*we are*	*going to church*
Tomorrow	*I am*	*going on holiday*

›Will future‹ wird nicht benutzt, wenn es um zukünftige feste Pläne geht.

2. Wann brauche ich das will future?

Das **will future** wird für die folgenden Situationen verwendet:

– Entscheidung jetzt
– Vorhersagen, Vermutungen
– Mit perhaps, maybe, I think usw.
– Um zu sagen, wo man in der Zukunft sein wird

a. Spontaner Entschluss (decision now)

Wird eine sofortige Entscheidung getroffen, wird das ›will future‹ benutzt. (›will future‹ wird oft am Telefon und in Meetings verwendet, wenn spontane Entscheidungen getroffen werden.). Decision now heißt: **I will DO something.**

Beispiele

You need money?	Ok, I **will** lend you some.
You are going to the cinema tonight?	Ok, I **will** come with you.
You have a problem?	Ok, I **will** help you.

b. Vorhersagen, Vermutungen (predictions, assumptions)

Wenn man über etwas spricht, das passieren könnte.

Beispiele

You look out of the window, dark clouds are forming: »I think it **will** rain tonight.«

Your team are playing well: »I think we will win.«

c. Mit probably/maybe, etc. + I think I will

Wenn man über etwas spricht, bei dem man nicht sicher ist: ›will future‹ verwenden (meistens mit ›probably‹, ›maybe‹, ›I think I will‹ etc.)

Beispiele

Maybe I **will** watch the match, I'm not sure.

I **will** probably stay in tonight. (zuhause bleiben)

I think I **will** go to the show tonight, but I'm not sure.

d. Um zu sagen, wo man in der Zukunft sein wird (To say where you think you will be in the future.)

This time tomorrow **I will be** in Rome.

This time next year **I will be** a millionaire.

Remember:
We DO NOT use ›will future‹ for fixed plans or activities!

~~I will meet John in the pub tonight.~~ I am meeting John in the pub tonight.

Point 15 – Progress test
Understand the will future

1. Will future

Decide which words are correct to finish the sentences, as in the example.
You look out of the window, it's very dark.
*I think **it will rain**/it is raining.*

1. You have plans to meet your girlfriend in the city tonight.
   I will meet/I am meeting Sue tonight.
2. You and your friend have booked a holiday in Italy next summer.
   We are going/we will go to Italy in July.
3. You might go to the cinema tonight, but you are not sure.
   Maybe I am going/will go to the cinema tonight.
4. You are moving to Spain in three months.
   I will move/am moving to Spain in three months.
5. Your partner comes home, cold and hungry.
   I make/will make you something to eat.
6. You meet your neighbour, his car has broken down. He needs to get to the city urgently.
   I give you/will give you a lift into the city.
7. You might go to Portugal for Christmas.
   I am going/might go to Portugal for Christmas.
8. You have plans to play football on Sunday with some old friends.
   I will play/am playing football at the weekend.
9. You will probably watch the big tonight.
   I will watch/might watch the big game tonight.
10. You have decided to paint the kitchen at the weekend.
    I will/am painting the kitchen at the weekend.

Point 16
Colour your English
(proverbs, expressions & colloquialisms)

»Buntes Englisch« (Sprichwörter, Ausdrücke und umgangssprachliche Redewendungen)

Die englische Sprache hat eine wunderbare Menge von Sprichwörtern, Redensarten und Ausdrücken, die jedem Wortschatz mehr Farbe verleihen können. Dieser Abschnitt ist ihnen gewidmet.

1. Idioms & colloquialisms in pictures

1. To skive off work
blaumachen

2. To go belly-up
schiefgehen

3. Looking for Hughie
kotzen

4. To throw a wobbly
ausrasten

5. Down in the dumps
niedergeschlagen

6. Taking the mickey
verăppeln

7. Done up like a kipper
übers Ohr gehauen

8. As pure as the driven snow
so unschuldig wie ein Engel sein

9. Like death warmed up
wie eine wandelnde Leiche aussehen

10. A cock up
Mist bauen

11. Don't see eye to eye
nicht in Übereinstimmung sein

12. To raise eyebrows
für (etwas) Stirnrunzeln sorgen

13. Rubbernecking
Gaffen

14. yellow
feige

15. lazy bones
stinkfaul

16. Lying through your back teeth
lügen wie ein Weltmeister

17. Pissing down
es pisst

18. As thick as two short planks
dumm wie Brot

19. Pigs might fly
Wenn Schweine fliegen könnten!

20. Blotto
rotzbesoffen

2. Nice idioms (nette Redewendungen)

1. Fall off the back of a lorry (vom Lastwagen fallen)

Das ist die britische Art zu sagen, dass du etwas erworben hast, das wahrscheinlich gestohlen wurde, oder dass du versuchst, etwas zu verkaufen, das gestohlen wurde oder ungesetzlich ist. Das amerikanische Äquivalent zu diesem Satz ist: ›fall off the back of a truck‹.

2. Do a runner (den Wirt um die Zeche prellen)

Wenn jemand ›einen Läufer macht‹, verlässt er einen Ort in Eile, um nicht für etwas bezahlen zu müssen (wie in einem Restaurant), oder flieht aus einer schwierigen Situation, um der Strafe zu entgehen.

3. For donkey's years (eine Ewigkeit)

Dieser Ausdruck bezieht sich auf die lange Lebensdauer des Tieres. Wenn jemand etwas ›for donkey's years‹ getan hat, hat er es für eine schrecklich lange Zeit getan.

4. If you'll pardon my French (Verzeih meine offene Rede)

›Pardon my French‹, also ›Entschuldige mein Französisch‹, ist eine informelle Entschuldigung für den Einsatz von Schimpfwörtern.

5. Has the cat got your tongue? (Hat es dir die Sprache verschlagen?)

Dies ist eine andere Art zu fragen: ›Warum bist du so still?‹

6. To have a one track mind (nur einspurig denken)

Dieser Ausdruck wird verwendet, um jemanden zu beschreiben, der nur an eine Sache denkt, meistens jemand, der von Sex besessen ist.

7. To bend over backwards (sich ein Bein ausreißen)

›To bend over backwards‹ bedeutet, alles zu tun, um jemandem zu helfen. Oft verwendet, um Enttäuschung auszudrücken: »I bent over backwards to help her, but she didn't appreciate it.«

8. To get up someone's nose (auf den Wecker gehen)

Jemanden wirklich nerven.

9. Washed out (verbraucht/erschöpft)

Psychisch und/oder geistig erschöpft.

10. To splash out (sich nicht lumpen lassen)

Eine Menge Geld ausgeben, um Dinge zu kaufen, vor allem Dinge, die man nicht wirklich braucht.

3. Weird & wacky expressions (seltsame und verrückte Ausdrücke)

Die wörtliche Bedeutung vieler Ausdrücke auf Englisch hat keine Ähnlichkeit mit ihrer tatsächlichen Bedeutung. Zum Beispiel bedeutet ›hit the sack‹ nicht ›schlag den Sack‹, sondern ›go to bed‹ (›Geh ins Bett!‹).

Dies ist eine **Sammlung von seltsamen und verrückten Ausdrücken**, ihren wörtlichen Übersetzungen und ihren tatsächlichen Bedeutungen.

1. Hot potato

A potato that has just come out of the oven

eine Kartoffel, die gerade aus dem Ofen gekommen ist

A topical, controversial subject

heißes Eisen

2. (To) go begging

To ask people for money

Leute um Geld bitten

To be available for one to take or claim

keinen Abnehmer finden

3. Don't give up your daytime job

Don't quit your job

Gib deinen Job nicht auf

You suck at what you do!

Du kannst das überhaupt nicht!

4. Talk of the devil

Talk about Satan

über den Teufel sprechen

Talk about someone and they are bound to appear

Wenn man vom Teufel spricht …

5. Hit the nail on the head

Do some DIY

basteln oder werken

Describe something perfectly

den Kern (der Sache) treffen

6. Miss the boat

Get to the harbour too late

zu spät am Hafen ankommen

Miss an opportunity

die Gelegenheit verpassen

7. Sit on the fence

Relax in the garden

auf dem Zaun sitzen

Refuse to make a decision or take sides

sich neutral verhalten

8. Hit the sack

Be violent towards a canvas bag

auf einen Sack einschlagen

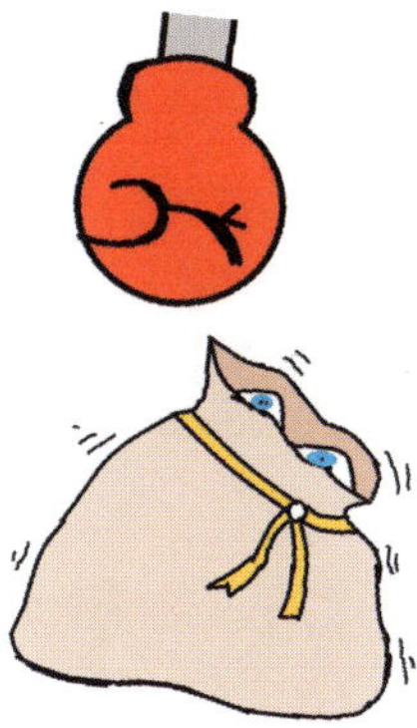

Go to bed

in die Falle gehen

9. Bite off more than you can chew

Overfill your mouth

mehr essen, als man kauen kann

Take on more than you can handle

sich übernehmen

10. To have a bun in the oven

Doing some baking

mit Backen beschäftigt sein

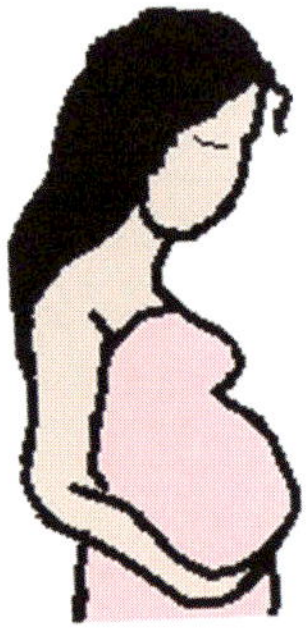

Pregnant

ein Brot im Ofen haben (schwanger sein)

11. Pushing up the daisies

Doing some gardening

Gartenarbeit machen

Dead

ins Gras beißen (tot sein)

12. Prickhead

A headful of pricks

Stichkopf

Arsehole

Scheißkerl

13. You are pulling my leg

You are annoying my lower limbs

Du ziehst an meinem Bein

You're joking with me

Du nimmst mich auf den Arm

14. It cost an arm and a leg

I paid in body parts

Es kostet einen Arm und ein Bein

It was very expensive

Es hat ein Vermögen gekostet

15. Don't count your chickens before they hatch

Who knows what's in the eggs?

Zähle deine Hühner nicht, bevor sie ihre Eier ausgebrütet haben

Don't make too many plans in advance

Man soll den Tag nicht vor dem Abend loben

Point 16 – Progress test
Colour your English

1. Colour your English

Choose the correct answer

1. **›Taking the mickey‹ means:**
   a. Making fun of someone b. Giving someone money

2. **›Yellow‹ means:**
   a. Blind b. Afraid

3. **›Done up like a kipper‹ means:**
   a. Fancily dressed b. Fooled

4. **›You are pulling my leg‹ means:**
   a. You are hurting me b. You are joking with me

5. **›Hit the sack‹ means:**
   a. Go to bed b. Hit someone

6. **A ›hot potato‹ is:**
   a. Too hot to handle b. A tricky subject

7. **›Fall off the back of a lorry‹ means:**
   a. Stolen b. Broken

8. **›Do a runner‹ means:**
   a. Do some exercise b. Run off without paying

9. **›For donkey's years‹ means:**
   a. A long time b. A short time

10. **›To bend over backwards‹ means**:
    a. To hurt yourself b. To be very helpful

Point 17

Use better words

Eine schneller und einfacher Weg, besser Englisch zu sprechen oder zu schreiben, besteht darin, bessere Wörter zu verwenden.

1. Using more advanced adverbs

(Verwenden von besseren Adverbien)

Dies sind Standardphrasen in E-Mails:

I am very sorry about the delay …

I am really sorry about what happened …

We are very excited about the new project …

›Very‹ und ›really‹ sind Adverbien, in diesem Fall beschreiben sie die Adjektive ›sorry‹ und ›excited‹.

Aber mit anspruchsvolleren Adverbien kann das eigene Englisch auf ein neues Level gebracht werden.

Vergleiche die folgenden Sätze:

I am very sorry.	*I am **terribly** sorry.*
We are very excited.	*We are **incredibly** excited.*
He was badly injured.	*He was **terribly** injured.*

In jedem Fall klingt der Satz rechts (mit dem anspruchsvolleren Adverb) besser.

Andere Beispiele für Verbesserungen mit Adverbien:

He is married.

*He is **happily** married.*

The roof was damaged.

*The roof was **badly** damaged.*

He is selfish.

*He is **terribly** selfish.*

She is pregnant.

*She is **heavily** pregnant.*

She is shy.

*She is **unbelievably** shy.*

Adverbs – important spelling rule
(Adverbien – wichtige Rechtschreibregel)

Adverbien werden normalerweise mit **-ly** am Ende eines Adjektivs gebildet. Zum Beispiel:

quick – quick**ly**

Bei Adjektiven, die auf -l oder -e enden, hängen wir einfach -ly an:

special + ly	- specially
terminal + ly	- terminally
literal + ly	- literally
nice + ly	- nicely
polite + ly	- politely

Es gibt natürlich einige Ausnahmen bzw. Besonderheiten:

true	–	truly
whole	–	wholly
due	–	duly
full	–	fully

Bei Adjektiven, die auf -y enden, entfernen wir -y und hängen -ily an:

crazy	–	crazily
happy	–	happily

Bei Adjektiven, die auf einen Konsonanten + le enden, entfernen wir -e und hängen -y an:

terrible	–	terribly
horrible	–	horribly
noble	–	nobly
idle	–	idly

Wenn das Adjektiv auf -ic endet, hängen wir -ally an:

ironic	–	ironically
enthusiastic	–	enthusiastically
realistic	–	realistically
Außer: public	–	publicly

Unregelmäßige Adverbien

Einige Adverbien sind unregelmäßig:

Adjective	Adverb	Example
fast	fast	The man is fast./He drives very fast.
good	well	Your English is good./You speak English well.

2. Using more advanced verbs

(Verwenden von besseren Verben)

Jeder kennt die Standardverben work, play, eat usw. Die Verwendung von schwierigeren und selteneren Verben kann die Sprache zusätzlich verbessern.

Hier ist eine Liste von Standardverben und Alternativvorschlägen.

verb	Alter-native(s) 1	Alter-native(s) 2
1. Let's **buy** it!	purchase	acquire
2. **Scatter** the seeds evenly.	spread/sow	strew
3. Did he **notice** you?	see/observe	heed/mark
4. He **promised** he'd do it. one's word	pledge	assure/give
5. Did the prisoner **escape**?	flee/skedaddle	bolt
6. **Fasten** the rope to the side.	tie/fix	tighten/secure
7. You must **obey** my orders.	follow/comply (with)	abide (by)/ observe
8. Don't **shout**, I'm not deaf!	holler/scream/ howl	yell/screech/ bawl
9. Don't **use** your fingers!	utilise	employ
10. I **work** like a dog.	travail/slog	labour
11. He **walks** everywhere.	stroll	amble
12. **Choose** your favourite.	select	pick
13. I've **hurt** my foot.	damage	injure
14. Ok, let's **begin**.	start/kick off	commence/ initiate
15. Will you **bet** on the race?	wager	punt/have a flutter

3. Using more advanced adjectives

(Verwendung von besseren Adjektiven)
Das gleiche gilt für Adjektiven.
Hier ist eine Liste von Standardadjektiven und Alternativvorschlägen.

Adjective	Alter-native(s) 1	Alter-native(s) 2
1. Her room is always **tidy**.	neat	orderly
2. That is very **thoughtful** of you.	caring	considerate
3. Ron is not very **sociable**.	outgoing	companionable

4. She is very **hard-working**.	conscientious	diligent
5. I always try to be **punctual**.	on time	on the dot
6. Samatha is very **intelligent**.	clever/sharp	smart/brainy
7. She keeps the place very **clean**.	immaculate/ spic and span	spotless/spruce
8. He's as **strong** as an ox.	powerful	forceful
9. It's **in working order**.	running/operative	functioning
10. It's a **common** complaint.	general	standard/usual
11. His new car is **big**.	massive/huge	gigantic/ enormous
12. Their prices are too **expensive**.	dear/costly	outrageous
13. It's a very **boring** pub.	dull/drab	dreary/dismal
14. The film was **exciting**.	shocking/ spine-tingling	thrilling/heady
15. The forest is a **quiet** place.	calm/still	tranquil/sedate
16. You seem **nervous**?	edgy/on edge/ flustered	jittery/jumpy
17. Sid is very **angry**.	disgruntled/ annoyed	cross/upset/ irked
18. She is very **honest**.	truthful/straight	sincere/faithful
19. These pillows are so **soft**.	fluffy	squishy
20. He is so **cowardly**.	craven/gutless	chicken/yellow

4. Prefixes

Eine andere gute Möglichkeit, das Vokabular zu erweitern, ist das Lernen von Präfixen. Präfixe ändern gewöhnlich die Bedeutung eines Wortes von positiv zu negativ oder wenden sie ins Gegenteil.

Beispiele

experienced – **in**experienced
mature – **im**mature
logical – **il**logical
ethical – **un**ethical

Es ist möglich, **not** vor diese Worte zu setzen, um die Negation oder das Gegenteil zu bilden. Aber alle diese Wörter können mit einem **prefix** verwendet werden, was die Bedeutung des Wortes völlig ändert. Es klingt auch besser.

He is not experienced.	He is inexperienced.
He is not mature.	He is immature.
He is not rational.	He is irrational.
It is not logical.	It is illogical.
It is not ethical.	It is unethical.

In jedem Fall klingen die Wörter, die Präfixe verwenden, besser!
Die am häufigsten verwendeten Präfixe und Wörter:

in-

acceptable/inacceptable	akzeptabel/inakzeptabel
accurate/inaccurate	genau/ungenau
appropriate/inappropriate	geeignet/ungeeignet
articulate/inarticulate	artikuliert/unartikuliert
audible/inaudible	hörbar/unhörbar
experienced/inexperienced	erfahren/unerfahren
visible/invisible	sichtbar/unsichtbar

im-

possible/impossible	möglich/unmöglich
mature/immature	reif/unreif
patient/impatient	geduldig/ungeduldig
partial/impartial	einseitig/unparteiisch
probable/improbable	wahrscheinlich/unwahrscheinlich

ir-

responsible/irresponsible	verantwortlich/unverantwortlich
regular/irregular	regelmäßig/unregelmäßig
repairable/irreparable	reparabel/irreparabel

il-

logical/illogical	logisch/unlogisch
legal/illegal	legal/illegal
literate/illiterate	belesen/analphabeten

un-

well/unwell	gesund/ungesund
able/unable	fähig/unfähig
aware/unaware	bewusst/unbewusst
helpful/unhelpful	hilfsbereit/nicht hilfreich
believable/unbelievable	glaubwürdig/unglaublich
safe/unsafe	sicher/unsicher
known/unknown	bekannt/unbekannt
kind/unkind	lieb/grausam
afraid/unafraid	ängstlich/furchtlos
fair/unfair	fair/unfair
willing/unwilling	willig/widerwillig
professional/unproffesional	professionell/unprofessionell

dis-

allow/disallow	erlauben/verweigern
appear/disappear	erscheinen/verschwinden
arm/disarm	bewaffnen/entwaffnen
like/dislike	mögen/nicht mögen
organised/disorganised	organisiert/desorganisiert

non-

smoker/nonsmoker	Raucher/Nichtraucher
addictive/nonaddictive	süchtig machend/nicht süchtig machend
payment/nonpayment	Zahlung/Nichtzahlung

Point 17 – Progress test
Use better words

1. Advanced adverbs

Use the adjectives in the brackets, in the correct form, to finish the sentences, as in the example.

*He is **happily** married. (happy)*

1. He was ______________ injured. (terrible)
2. The roof was ______________ damaged. (bad)
3. He is ______________ selfish. (awful)
4. She is ______________ shy. (unbelievable)
5. She is ______________ pregnant. (heavy)
6. The weather was ______________ hot. (extreme)
7. My hotel was ______________ expensive. (incredible)
8. The meeting was ______________ useful. (fair)
9. He was ______________ surprised. (pleasant)
10. My flight was ______________ delayed. (slight)

2. Prefixes

Use the word in brackets and the correct prefix to complete the sentences.

1. Many politicians are very __________________. (professional)
2. He doesn't make a lot of sense, he's __________________. (logical)
3. She is chaotic and extremely __________________. (organised)
4. I was __________________ of any problems. (aware)
5. I think ›teach' is an __________________ verb. (regular)
6. Tom is always so __________________. (patient)
7. She is very childish and __________________. (mature)
8. Those terms are totally __________________ to me. (acceptable)
9. He is not a good speaker, rather __________________. (articulate)
10. She was __________________ to compromise. (willing)

Point 18

Avoid making the biggest mistakes

Dieser Abschnitt gibt einen umfassenden Überblick über die 15 schlimmsten Fehler, die beim Englischsprechen gemacht werden.

1. Say or tell?

Say something but you **tell someone** something.

Tom **told me** he was ill. **Tom said** he was ill.

2. Doing something now (present progressive)

Für das present progressive braucht man **is/are/am + -ing**.

Is/are/am können nicht ohne **-ing** verwendet werden, **-ing** kann nicht ohne is/are/am verwendet werden.

I **am doing** something. He **is going** somewhere. We **are talking**.

3. He/she/it, ein s muss mit!

Dies ist immer noch eine der größten Fehlerquellen auf allen Ebenen.

I play football. He **plays** football. She **plays** badminton.

4. Mixed tenses

last week – is the **simple past**
Last week I **went** to Spain.
I have been ... – is the **present perfect**
I **have been** to Spain.

5. Preference verbs + -ing

Bei der Verwendung von Verben, die beschreiben, was man mag (Vorlieben), wird das nächste Verb (Bezugswort) normalerweise mit der ing-Form gebildet.

I like doing something.	–	I **like watching** TV.
I hate doing something.	–	I **hate washing** up.
I love doing something.	–	I **love shopping** in the city.

6. Watch something/look at something

Watch für eine lange Zeit ansehen
I **watched** the game, I **watched** the film.
Look at für eine kurze Zeit (an)sehen
Look at that pretty girl, **look at** that bird in the garden.

7. Hear or listen (to)?

Hier gilt das gleiche Prinzip wie bei **look/watch** – die Dauer der Handlung ist entscheidend!

Hear wenn ich etwas **für eine kurze Zeit** (ggf. zufällig) höre.
Listen to wenn ich etwas/jemanden(m) **für eine längere Zeit** (zu)höre.

I **listened to** music **all night.**
I **listened to** the radio for a while before I went to sleep.
I **heard a noise** in the garden.
The sports car **drove past** and I **could hear** the techno music.

8. Truth or true?

Achte darauf, Nomen und Adjektive auseinanderzuhalten und in der richtigen Situation anzuwenden:

He doesn't know **the truth**.

The truth is **the noun**.

It is **true**.

True is **an adjective**.

9. Don't or doesn't?

I do/you do/we do/they do
I don't/you don't/we don't/they don't

He/she/it does
He/she/it doesn't

10. Normal or normally?

Ein Adjektiv beschreibt ein Nomen genauer.
Ein Adverb beschreibt ein Verb (wie man etwas macht).

Paul is a **normal person**

adjective noun

It was a **normal day**

adjective noun

Paul **normally goes** to work at eight

adverb verb

Pete **normally eats** lunch in the canteen

adverb verb

11. Why ›terribly sorry‹?

Ein Adverb kann auch ein Adjektiv näher beschreiben (wie leid tut es jemandem: sehr, wirklich, extrem etc.)

I am **terribly sorry**.

adverb adjective

He is **extremely happy**.

I am terribly sorry, they just said they wanted us to come over for lunch …

12. Interesting or interested?

Das **-ing** am Ende sagt uns, wie etwas ist (Zustand).

Das **-ed** am Ende sagt uns, wie sich jemand fühlt.

What is it?	How does someone feel about it?
Chemistry is **interesting**.	I am **interested** in chemistry.
The meeting was **boring**.	He was really **bored**.
The game was **exciting**.	He was **excited**.

13. Using the wrong words

Achte darauf, Verben und Substantive auseinanderzuhalten und in der richtigen Situation anzuwenden:

Verben beschreiben, was jemand tut.

Nomen (Substantive) beschreiben Personen oder Dinge (greifbar oder abstrakt).

He **instructed** me to move my car.	He gave me **instructions**.
They **delivered** the goods on Friday.	We got **the delivery** on Friday.
He **commented** on my clothes.	He made nice **comments**.
We **agreed** on a price.	We came to **an agreement**.

14. A or an?

Die Grundregel ist:

a + consonant	a beach	a pig	a bear
an + vowel	an ape	an egg	an umbrella

Ausnahmen

a. Bei Wörtern, die mit u anfangen, das wie ein j ausgesprochen wird, verwendet man **a**:

unit/university – pronounced junit/juniversity – **a unit/a university**

b. Bei Wörtern, die mit einem stummen h beginnen, verwendet man **an**:

honest/hour – pronounced onest/our – **an** (h)onest man/**an** (h)onest mistake

c. Bei Wörtern, die mit o beginnen, das wie w ausgesprochen wird, benötigt man **a**:

one – pronounced **wone** – *therefore* **a** one-legged man

once – pronounced **wonce** – *therefore* **a** once in a lifetime experience

15. Reflexive pronouns

Reflexivpronomen werden als direktes Objekt verwendet, wenn das Objekt das Subjekt des Verbs ist:

I am teaching **myself** to play the piano.
Be careful with that knife. **You** might cut **yourself**.
Ron is excited. **He's** just bought **himself** a new car.
Singular: me – **myself**, you – **yourself**, him – **himself**, her – **herself**
Plural: you – **yourselves**, we – **ourselves**, they – **themselves**

Point 18 – Progress test Avoid making the biggest mistakes

1. Avoid making the biggest mistakes

Complete the sentences by choosing the correct word(s) in the brackets.

1. Tom ________ he was really tired. (said/told)
2. Don't ________ me, let me guess. (say/tell)
3. John ________ in a chair. (is sitting/sitting)
4. Eric ________ cricket every Saturday. (plays/play)
5. Last week I ________ to Holland. (went/have been)
6. I ________ been to Africa. (have/has)
7. I like ________. (read/reading)
8. I love ________. (cooking/cook)
9. I hate ________ tax. (paying/pay)
10. I don't mind ________. (clean/cleaning)
11. Did you ________ the game last night? (look/watch)
12. Do you ________ sport on TV? (watch/look)
13. He said the gold was ________. (real/really)

14. That is simply not ________. (truth/true)
15. I like ________ to ________ music. (listening/hearing/classic/classical)
16. It is ________ to cheat the taxman. (normal/normally)
17. Paul doesn't ________ drink alcohol. (normal/normally)
18. Be ________. (careful/carefully)
19. He is ________ unhappy. (extreme/extremely)
20. He was ________ shocked. (real/really)
21. Are you ________ sport? (interesting/interested)
22. Do you find politics ________? (interested/interesting)
23. Just follow my ________. (instruct/instructions)
24. Sorry, but I don't ________ with you. (agree/agreement)
25. There is ________ big hotel in the centre. (a/an)
26. I am proud to be ________ European. (a/an)
27. Sue is married to ________ African. (a/an)
28. The pound is ________ unit of currency. (a/an)
29. There is ________ university in the city. (a/an)
30. He was ________ old man. (a/an)

Point 19

Make better small talk

In jeder Sprache ist Smalltalk eine schwierige Aufgabe, besonders wenn man jemanden zum ersten Mal trifft. Es gibt keine Zauberformel für erfolgreichen Smalltalk, aber es gibt einige allgemeine Richtlinien, denen man folgen sollte.

1. Taboo

Im Allgemeinen sind die folgenden Themen tabu, es sei denn, die andere Person spricht das Thema an:

sex	politics
money	personal problems
terrorism	death
weight	salary
religion	ambition

2. Small talk tips

a. Ask open-ended questions

Stelle offene Fragen, d. h. Fragen, die mehr als ein einfaches ›yes‹ oder ›no‹ erfordern. Fragen mit **why** und **how** sind gute Beispiele, etwa ›Why are you travelling to New York?‹ Darauf sollte man eine ausführlichere Antwort bekommen als auf: ›Is this your first time in New York?‹

b. Talk less and listen more

Zuhören, was jemand sagt, kann viele andere Möglichkeiten für ein Gespräch eröffnen. Fragen über Kinder können zu Gesprächen über den Bildungsstand in einem Land, die Universitätsausbildung, den Unterrichtsstandard usw. führen.

c. Keep up with current events

Small Talk über aktuelle Nachrichten, Sport, Gesellschaft oder Politik (es sei denn, die Politik ist sehr umstritten).

d. Share an anecdote about your day

Gab es Stau? Gab es beim Check-in lange Warteschlangen? Wie war das Mittagessen? Beim Smalltalk geht es darum, die kleinen Dinge zu teilen.

e. Ask about films or books

Manchmal kann dies der Beginn einer langen Unterhaltung sein, wenn man denselben Film gesehen oder kürzlich dasselbe Buch gelesen hat.

3. Small talk/travelling phrases – English/German

Greetings & introductions	**Begrüßen & (sich) vorstellen**
English	**German**
Pleased to meet you.	*Es freut mich, Sie/dich kennenzulernen.*
Pleased to see you again.	*Es freut mich, Sie wiederzusehen.*
My name is John Simmons.	*Ich heiße John Simmons.*
What do you do for a living?	*Was machen Sie beruflich?*
I am an English trainer.	*Ich bin Englischlehrer.*
What company do you work for?	*Für welche Firma arbeiten Sie?*
I work at Lexis Languages.	*Ich arbeite bei Lexis Languages.*
How are you?	*Wie geht es Ihnen?*
Fine, thanks.	*Danke, gut.*
Where are you from?	*Woher kommen Sie?*
I come from Windsor.	*Ich komme aus Windsor.*
Where do you live?	*Wo wohnen Sie?*
I live in Cologne.	*Ich wohne in Köln.*

May I introduce you to David Pollard?	*Darf ich Ihnen David Pollard vorstellen?*
How long are you staying in Germany/Austria/ Switzerland?	*Wie lange bleiben Sie in Deutschland/ Österreich/der Schweiz?*
I am here for one week/two weeks/three weeks.	*Ich bleibe eine Woche/zwei Wochen/drei Wochen.*

socialising	**In Kontakt kommen**
Would you like something to drink?	*Möchten Sie etwas trinken?*
Can I offer you a drink?	*Kann ich Ihnen etwas zu trinken anbieten?*
How do you take your coffee?	*Wie trinken Sie Ihren Kaffee?*
Please take a seat.	*Bitte nehmen Sie Platz.*
I would like to invite you for dinner.	*Ich möchte Sie zum Essen einladen.*
Are you available this evening for dinner?	*Haben Sie heute Abend Zeit, mit mir Essen zu gehen?*
How was your journey?	*Wie war Ihre Reise?*
In which hotel are you staying?	*In welchem Hotel übernachten Sie?*

farewells	**Sich verabschieden**
It was nice meeting you.	*Es war nett, Sie kennenzulernen.*
See you later.	*Bis später.*
I look forward to seeing you again.	*Ich freue mich, Sie wiederzusehen.*

Misunderstandings	**Wenn man etwas nicht verstanden hat**
I don't understand.	*Ich verstehe (Sie) nicht.*
Can you repeat that please?	*Können Sie das bitte wiederholen?*
Can you say it again?	*Können Sie das nochmal wiederholen?*

Do you speak English?	*Sprechen Sie Englisch?*
I only speak a little German.	*Ich spreche nur wenig Deutsch.*
Can you translate that please?	*Können Sie das übersetzen?*
I'm sorry? (if you don't hear something)	*Entschuldigung, ich habe Sie nicht verstanden! (gehört)*
Sorry. (for a mistake)	*Entschuldigung!/Es tut mir leid!*
No problem!	*Kein Problem!/Keine Ursache!*
Can you speak slowly?	*Können Sie (etwas) langsamer sprechen?*
Write it down, please!	*Schreiben Sie es bitte auf!*
I don't know!	*Ich weiß (es) nicht!*
I have no idea.	*Ich habe keine Ahnung.*
What's that called in German?	*Wie heißt das auf Deutsch?*
What does ›teuer‹ mean in English?	*Was bedeutet ›teuer‹ auf Englisch?*
How do you say ›please‹ in German?	*Wie sagt man ›please‹ auf Deutsch?*
What is this?	*Was ist das?*
My German is bad.	*Mein Deutsch ist schlecht.*
I need to practice my German.	*Ich muss mein Deutsch ausprobieren.*
Don't worry!	*Keine Sorge!/Kein Problem!*

General expressions & words	**Allgemeine Ausdrücke & Wörter**
good/bad/so-so.	*gut/schlecht/so la-la*
big/small	*groß/klein*
today/now	*heute/jetzt*
tomorrow/yesterday	*morgen/gestern*
yes/no	*ja/nein*
Here you go! (when giving something)	*Bitte sehr!/Bitte schön!*
Do you like it?	*Gefällt's Ihnen/dir?*
I really like it!	*Mir gefällt es sehr gut!*
I'm hungry/thirsty.	*Ich habe Hunger/Durst.*

In the morning/evening/at night	*morgens/abends/nachts*
this/that/here/there	*dies(es/er/e)/das/hier/dort*
me/you/him/her	*ich/Sie/er/sie*
Really?	*wirklich?/echt?*
Look!	*Guck (mal)/Schau (mal)!*
Hurry up!	*Beeil dich!/Beeilen Sie sich!*
What? Where?	*Was?/Wo?*
What time is it?	*Wieviel Uhr ist es?/Wie spät ist es?*
It's 10 o'clock.	*Es ist zehn Uhr.*
Give me this!	*Gib mir das!*
I feel sick.	*Ich fühle mich nicht wohl.*
I need a doctor.	*Ich brauche einen Arzt.*
one, two, three	*eins, zwei, drei*
four, five, six	*vier, fünf, sechs*
seven, eight, nine, ten	*sieben, acht, neun, zehn*
I'm looking for a pharmacy.	*Ich suche eine Apotheke.*
Are there any side effects?	*Gibt es irgendwelche Nebenwirkungen?*
My doctor said …	*Mein Arzt sagte (mir) …*

More informal phrases	**Formlosere Wendungen**
My (telephone) number is …	*Meine Telefonnummer ist …*
You can call me at any time	*Du kannst mich jederzeit anrufen.*
You can send me a text message.	*Du kannst mir eine SMS schicken.*
You can write me an e-mail	*Du kannst mir eine E-Mail schreiben.*
Why didn't I think of that?	*Warum ist mir das nicht eingefallen?*
I noticed that, too.	*Das ist mir auch aufgefallen.*
The telephone bill is due.	*Die Telefonrechnung ist fällig.*
Enjoy the meal!	*Guten Appetit!*
I'm bored.	*Mir ist langweilig.*
Be quiet!	*Sei ruhig/still!*

Get lost!	*Verschwinde!*
What's wrong with you?	*Was hast du?*
Are you crazy?	*Spinnst du?*
Leave me alone!	*Lass mich in Ruhe!*
I miss you	*Ich vermisse dich.*
I love you!	*Ich liebe dich!*
I like you	*Ich mag dich./Ich habe dich gern.*
Are you free tomorrow evening?	*Hast du morgen Abend Zeit?*
I would like to invite you to dinner	*Ich möchte dich zum Abendessen einladen.*
You look beautiful!	*Du siehst schön aus!*
Can you tell me more about you?	*Kannst du mir mehr über dich erzählen?*
I'm single.	*Ich bin Single.*
I'm married.	*Ich bin verheiratet.*
I'm not interested!	*Interessiert mich nicht!*
Can I have your phone number?	*Kann ich deine Telefonnummer haben?*
Would you like to go for a walk?	*Möchtest du spazieren gehen?*
I'm just kidding.	*Ich mache nur Spaß.*
I'm serious.	*Ich meine es Ernst.*
I'm vegetarian.	*Ich bin Vegetarier.*
I'm vegan.	*Ich bin Veganer.*
I don't eat pork.	*Ich esse kein Schweinefleisch.*
I don't drink alcohol.	*Ich trinke keinen Alkohol.*
My God!	*Liebe Güte!*
Oh gosh!	*Ach je!*

Point 19 – Progress test
Make better small talk

1. Make better small talk

Complete the sentences by choosing the correct word(s) in the brackets.

1. What do you do for a ________? (living/life)
2. Can you speak ________, please? (slowly/slow)
3. ________ like something to drink? (Do you/Would you)
4. Where ________you from? (are/is)
5. How was your ________? (travel/journey)
6. Are there any side ________? (efforts/effects)
7. Pleased to ________ you. (meeting/meet)
8. How do you say ›please‹ in ________? (Germany/German)
9. I'm ________. (boring/bored)
10. It was nice ________you. (meet/meeting)
11. I'm not ____________! (interested/interesting)
12. I'm ________. (married/marry)
13. I'm ________. (hunger/hungry)
14. Hurry ________! (up/on)
15. I ________understand. (don't/not)
16. In which hotel are you ________? (staying/stay)
17. I would like to ________ you for dinner. (invite/invest)
18. I don't ________ alcohol. (drink/eat)
19. Pleased to ________ you again. (seeing/see)
20. My ________ is bad. (Germany/German)

Point 20

Cut the crap

Und das Wichtigste am Schluss, um zu verhindern, dass immer wieder die gleichen Fehler gemacht werden:

… **just don't do** any of the following – bitte vermeide diesen Unsinn …

1. He don't	**He doesn't**
2. He/she play	**He/she plays**
3. I don't can	**I can't**
4. We meet us	**See you …**
5. I doing something	**I am doing something**
6. A piano-player	**A piano player**
7. That's to much	**That's too much**
8. Its only a game	**It's only a game**

9. Yesterday I do something	Yesterday I did something
10. Make work	Do work
11. Look sport	Watch sport
12. Make holiday	Go on holiday
13. Drive careful	Drive carefully
14. Terrible expensive	Terribly expensive
15. Congratulation	Congratulations
16. I know you for years	I have known you for years
17. Since 10 years	For ten years
18. One and a half hour	One and a half hours
19. Two childs	Two children
20. I hurt me	I hurt myself

Points 1–20 Abschlusstest

1. Abschlusstest

In each case choose the correct answer.

1. Time flys/flies.
2. It's defekt/defect.
3. I having/I am having a party on Saturday.
4. Paul is go/going to a party now.
5. He do/does a lot of business with Japan.
6. Did/Have you ever swum in the ocean?
7. Has/Have you ever driven a sports car?
8. Where does/do your parents live?
9. Is/Are Paul coming to the party?
10. Two tomatoes/tomato.
11. Two bus/buses.
12. Five sheep/sheeps.
13. Two wifes/wives.
14. Making mistakes is really frustrating/frustrated.
15. I get frustrated/frustrating when I can't express myself.
16. Put/Take off your coat.
17. I am not afraid off/of snakes.
18. He rides on/at his horse.
19. She got married with/at 18.
20. Yesterdays/yesterday's paper.
21. A years'/a year's salary.
22. A minutes/a minute's silence.

23. I like walking in the Hyde Park/in Hyde Park.

24. I don't like walking in the park/in park.

25. I picked up my recipe/prescription.

26. My plane was cancelled/delayed by an hour.

27. Never lend/borrow money from a friend.

28. We always control/check each delivery.

29. The English kitchen/cuisine isn't very good.

30. They got lost in the dessert/desert and died.

31. Always proof/check your car tyres regularly.

32. Maybe I am going/will go to the cinema tonight.

33. I will move/am moving to Spain in three months.

34. Yellow means:

a. Blind b. Afraid

35. Blotto means:

a. Drunk b. Tired

36. I like read/reading.

37. I love cooking/cook.

38. I hate paying/pay tax.

39. I hurt me/myself.

40. It's terrible/terribly expensive.

Progress tests – Solutions & assessments

Es gibt einen Punkt für jede richtige Antwort oder für jeden gefundenen Fehler. Die Ergebnisse sollten überprüft (Punktzahl) und die Anweisungen unter jeder Lösung verfolgt werden.

Point 1 – Progress test Improve your spelling

Maximale Punktzahl: 40

1. Doing Business in the Global Market

One **aspekt (aspect)** of doing business that I don't enjoy is the speed at which things have to be done. **Befor (Before)** we had **satellits (satellites)**, e-mail and smart phones, life was much easier.

Nowadays we have to **decid (decide)** on the spot, make quick decisions and simply do not have time to think. My colleague **do (does)** a lot of business overseas, I deal with the German market. He **go (goes)** to America quite a lot, in fact he **cross (crosses)** the Atlantic nearly every month. I usually **flies** on business about once a year, but he **flys (flies)** regularly. But I can't complain. At the moment I am earning a lot of money, which is lucky **becaus (because)** my wife's hobby is **shoping (shopping)**.

Time flys

Last week I looked at my **kalendar (calendar)** and couldn't **believ (believe)** it was nearly Christmas – time **flys (flies)**. It only seems like last week that I was on my summer holiday. It was great to go **dancing (dancing)** every night, **naping (napping)** by the pool in the afternoon and **runing (running)** on the beach every morning. I went **fishhing (fishing)** twice, even tried a little bit of **divving (diving)**.

Punktzahl ____ /20

2. Most misspelled words	Corrected words
1. **Its** raining again.	**it's**
2. **Your** so boring.	**you're**
3. They don't like **there** teacher.	**their**
4. I didn't **acheive** much at school.	**achieve**
5. I will **definitly** see you tomorrow.	**definitely**
6. The course was good in the **begining**.	**beginning**
7. I don't **belive** you.	**believe**
8. Will we get there **befor** six?	**before**
9. He has no **respekt** for his teachers.	**respect**
10. **Buisness** has been really bad this year.	**business**
11. He is nearly **fourty** years old.	**forty**
12. Do you know what happend?	**happened**
13. I **realy** don't know.	**really**
14. **Therefor** we need a new computer.	**therefore**
15. I **truely** hate my boss.	**truly**
16. I don't like **politicans**.	**politicians**
17. My **collegue** is very lazy.	**colleague**
18. That is a **seperate** issue.	**separate**
19. Write the appointment on the **calender**.	**calendar**
20. Our **goverment** is terrible.	**government**

Punktzahl ____ /20

Gesamtpunktzahl		
1.		
2.		
Total		/40

Weniger als 20 Fehler gefunden	20–29 Fehler gefunden	30–39 Fehler gefunden	Alle Fehler gefunden
Ach je! Punkt 1 sollte erneut durchgearbeitet werden.	Fast die Hälfte der Fehler wurden gefunden. Mehr Konzentration ist erforderlich.	Gut gemacht, aber die Fehler, die nicht gefunden wurden, müssen in Zukunft vermieden werden. Das macht den Unterschied zwischen gutem und sehr gutem Englisch aus.	Herzlichen Glückwünsch! Die Messlatte liegt jetzt hoch.

Point 2 – Progress test
Use the right verbs

Maximale Punktzahl: 35

1. Right or wrong?

1. Can you **make** some coffee to wake us up?
2. If you **make** a mistake, cross it out.
3. Let's **go on** a bike trip on Sunday!
4. I took many photos on holiday. ✓
5. He **donated** his bonus to Oxfam.
6. I can **do** business with her.
7. I get up at six o'clock. ✓
8. Do you **watch** a lot of television?
9. Does your wife **do** a lot of sport?
10. I'm listening to my new CD. ✓

Punktzahl ______ /10

2. Do

1. **Do** you live in a big city you?
2. What do you **do**?
3. **Does** he like his job?
4. **Do** you travel a lot in your job?
5. **Did** you watch the game last night?
6. **Do** you work for a big company?
7. Where **do** your parents live?
8. **Did** you go to Spain last week?
9. How are you **doing**?
10. What is that man **doing**?
11. Are you **doing** a marathon again?
12. **Do** you have any children?
13. What **does** your daughter do?
14. **Did** you pick your daughter's name?
15. What **does** your wife do?

Punktzahl ______ **/15**

3. Verbs

1. **Did** you do your homework yesterday?
2. Oh no, I **made** six mistakes in my test!
3. Paul is **baking** a pizza. It smells great!
4. Steve **did** a French course in 1989.
5. I **had** a party on Saturday.
6. Paul is **going** to a party now.
7. He **does** a lot of business with Japan.
8. I always **eat** breakfast at seven.

9. Paul **does** sport.
10. Are you **making** a cake?

Punktzahl ___ **/10**

Gesamtpunktzahl	
1.	
2.	
Total	**/35**

Weniger als 10 Punkte	**Zwischen 11–24 Punkte**	**25–32 Punkte**	**33–35 Punkte**
Ach je! Rechtschreibung ist schwerig. Dieser Abschnitt muss erneut ausgeführt werden.	Zu viele Regeln wurden nicht gelernt. Dieser Abschnitt sollte erneut bearbeitet werden und der Test erneut durchgeführt werden.	Ziemlich gut, aber ein wenig mehr Übung und Konzentration ist erforderlich.	Herzlichen Glückwünsch! Die Messlatte liegt jetzt hoch.

Point 3 – Progress test
Ask the right questions

Maximale Punktzahl: 30

1. Finish the sentences

1. **Does** she still live in London?
2. **Does** he work in the city?
3. **Does** she play volleyball?

4. **Is** she working in Spain?
5. Did you **speak** English yesterday?
6. **Have** you ever played squash?
7. **Has** he ever visited Madrid?
8. **Have** you ever eaten kangaroo?
9. Are you **reading** a good book?
10. **Are** we going now?
11. **Has** she left?
12. **Have** you ever swum in the ocean?
13. **Have** you ever driven a sports car
14. **Is** he going to the supermarket?
15. **Has** John ever bungee jumped?
16. **Did** you speak English yesterday?
17. Has Sue ever **ridden** a donkey?
18. **Have** you ever broken a leg?
19. Has he ever **broken** a bone?
20. How long have you **been** ill?
21. How long **have** you worked here?
22. How long have you **known** your wife?
23. How long **been** he worked here?
24. **Does** your wife speak English?
25. **Did** you speak to Syd yesterday?
26. **Are** you doing your housework?
27. **Is** that someone at the door?
28. Where **do** your parents live?
29. **Is** Paul coming to the party?
30. **Have** you spoken to him?

Gesamtpunktzahl ______ /30

Weniger als 10 Punkte	11–15 Punkte	15–24 Punkte	25–30 Punkte
Die Frage muss gestellt werden … Muss dieser Abschnitt wiederholt werden?	Zu viele Fehler. Dieser Abschnitt sollte erneut bearbeitet und der Test erneut durchgeführt werden.	Ziemlich gut. Der nächste Level ist in Sichtweite.	Herzlichen Glückwünsch! Mach weiter so!

Point 4 – Progress test
Get to know your capital letters

Maximale Punktzahl: 26

1. E-mail

Dear **J**ohn

Thank you for your **e**-mail. I am disappointed about yesterday's **m**eeting. But we have to find a **s**olution. I phoned **A**lan yesterday, maybe he will spend more money on the **p**roject. I also asked **T**racey to send me some **i**nformation from the **L**ondon **o**ffice. I have a **m**eeting with **T**im on **M**onday and with **J**ohn at the beginning of **O**ctober.

I will keep you informed about the **s**ituation.

Best wishes

Joe

Punktzahl ____ /16

2. Right or wrong?

1. Let's go to the pub tonight.	**Correct!**
2. Who paid for your tickets?	**Correct!**
3. He speaks German and Dutch.	**Correct!**
4. The holiday Inn is on East Road.	**Wrong**! The **H**oliday **I**nn is on East Road.

5. i like beer, but i don't like wine.	**Wrong! I** like beer, but **I** don't like wine.
6. There were 20 Men in the house.	**Wrong**! There were 20 **m**en in the house.
7. Would you like to come to my party?	**Correct!**
8. Hamburgers are popular in America.	**Correct!**
9. Do you like my Song?	**Wrong**! Do you like my **s**ong?
10. I'm listening to the Radio.	**Wrong**! I'm listening to the **r**adio.

Punktzahl ______ **/10**

Gesamtpunktzahl

1.		
2.		
Total		**/26**

Weniger als 10 Punkte	**11–21 Punkte**	**22–25 Punkte**	**26 Punkte**
Jemals von ›capital punishment‹ gehört? Punkt 4 sollte erneut durchgearbeitet werden.	Zwischen einem Viertel und der Hälfte aller Fehler wurde gefunden. Das bedeutet, dass mindestens die Hälfte nicht gefunden wurde!	Gut gemacht. Trotzdem noch Luft nach oben.	Well done!

Point 5 – Progress test
Is it singular or plural?

Maximale Punktzahl: 32

1. Plurals test

book	**books**	scarf	**scarves**	box	**boxes**
shelf	**shelves**	man	**men**	class	**classes**
mouse	**mice**	child	**children**	party	**parties**
family	**families**	woman	**women**	hobby	**hobbies**
leaf	**leaves**	watch	**watches**	tooth	**teeth**
tomato	**tomatoes**	bus	**buses**	sheep	**sheep**
wife	**wives**	fox	**foxes**	knife	**knives**

Punktzahl ____ **/21**

2. Spot the mistake

Sentences	Mistake(s)
1. There was a woman in the car with two **mens**.	**men**
2. I need **a** new jeans.	**new jeans**
3. David is married and has three **childs**.	**children**
4. Do you have many **friend** in this town?	**friends**
5. I like your **trouser**. Where did you get **it**?	**trousers/them**
6. **This** scissors are not sharp.	**these**
7. Some people **is** always late.	**are**
8. The police **is** looking for the criminals.	**are**
9. I need my glasses, but I can't find **it**.	**them**
10. My **foots** are cold.	**feet**

Punktzahl ____ **/11**

Gesamtpunktzahl	
1.	
2.	
Total	/32

Weniger als 15 Punkte	16–20 Punkte	21–31 Punkte	32 Punkte
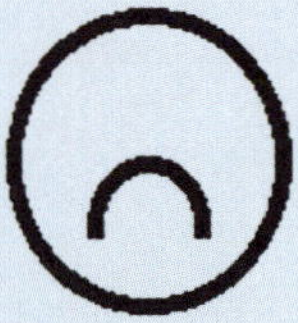	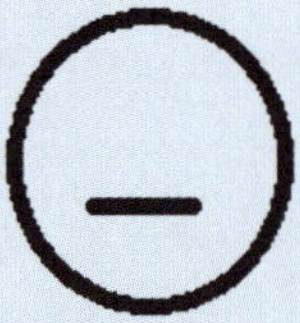		

Point 6 – Progress test
Get to grips with adjectives & adverbs

Maximale Punktzahl: 21

1. Choose the correct word

Next week I am going on my first business trip to Australia. I am very **excited** about it. I think it will be a **fascinating** trip because I will meet a lot of the people I have been working with for the last few years. The plane journey is about 18 hours, which I think will be very **tiring**. I am very **interested** in seeing the Australian way of doing business. I am a little bit **worried** about speaking English. My English isn't very good. I will be **surprised** if I understand everything at the meetings. Sometimes I find it really **frustrating** when I speak to my Australian colleagues, because I don't understand them and they don't understand me. We all get very **frustrated**.

The offices in Australia are **amazing**. They are situated next to a big lake, the view from the offices is wonderful. I don't think I will be **bored** during my stay because I have a lot of meetings planned. But I think I will be **exhausted** when I get back. I have spoken to the boss in Australia many times, he seems a very **amusing** guy. Sometimes I am **embarrassed** because my English is so bad, but he doesn't get **annoyed**. Sometimes, when I think about my first meeting, I feel quite **terrified**. But I'm sure it will be a **fulfilling** trip.

Punktzahl [ ] /16

2. Using adverbs (Possible answers)

1. Your colleague finishes a job in record time.	You say: **I'm absolutely** delighted.
2. The restaurant is not expensive.	You say: I'm **pleasantly** surprised.
3. You are very, very tired.	You say: I'm **extremely/terribly** exhausted!
4. You are very angry with someone.	You say: **incredibly/terribly/extremely** displeased!
5. You win first prize in a competition.	You say: I'm **pleasantly/extremely** surprised!

Punktzahl [ ] /5

Gesamtpunktzahl

1. [ ]

2. [ ]

Total [ ] /21

Weniger als 10 Punkte	11–15 Punkte	16–20 Punkte	21 Punkte
Ist das *depressing* oder *depressed*?	Es wird sehr *interesting* sein, diesen Abschnitt noch einmal zu machen …	Ziemlich gut. Der nächste Abschnitt sollte *fascinating* sein!	Gute Arbeit! *Onwards and upwards!*

Point 7 – Progress test
Learn your prepositions!
Maximale Punktzahl: 40

1. How good are your prepositions now?

1. Paul is married **to** my sister.
2. They are always talking **about** me behind my back.
3. I will see you **next** Wednesday.
4. He threw the ball **to** me and I caught it.
5. She was so angry, she threw a plate **at** me.
6. Shall we go **to** the restaurant tonight?
7. He went **into/in** the changing room and changed **into** his wetsuit.
8. Let's go **through** the schedule one more time.
9. This car is exactly the same **as** ours.
10. Can you look **after** my dog for two hours tonight?
11. He took **off** his coat and put **on** his shoes.
12. I am not afraid **of** snakes.
13. He rides **on** his horse.
14. She got married **at** 18.
15. Let's go **on** foot
16. He's staying **at** Bill's.
17. He is staying **with** Paula.
18. I was bitten **by** a cat.
19. That is very kind **of** you.
20. Listen **to** my new CD.

Punktzahl ______ **/20**

2. Time prepositions

1. Shall we have a party **on** your birthday?
2. I'll see you **at** 10 o'clock.
3. We can meet **next** Thursday.
4. I saw Bob **last** week.
5. I play chess **on/every** Sunday.
6. He fell asleep **during** the film.
7. Please deliver the goods **by/on** Wednesday.
8. I have to stay here **until** 12 o'clock.
9. I have been working here **for** 11 years.
10. Did you get many eggs **at** Easter?
11. I got married 13 years **ago**.
12. I have been working here **since** 1988.
13. Did you go to church **on** Easter Sunday?
14. Were you **on** holiday?
15. Did it snow **at** Christmas?
16. The cat always goes out **at** night.
17. Did you see your family **on** Christmas Day?
18. I had a cup of tea when I got **home**.
19. The ambulance arrived **in/after** five minutes.
20. The market is on **from** Friday **until** Sunday.

Punktzahl ____ /20

Gesamtpunktzahl		
1.		
2.		
Total		/40

Weniger als 25 Punkte	26–34 Punkte	35–39 Punkte	40 Punkte
Sein oder nicht sein? Nochmal machen, oder?	Immer noch ein wenig verwirrt mit den Präpositionen.	Fast perfekt. Versuch es weiter!	Beeindruckend!

Point 8 – Progress test Use the apostrophe properly

Maximale Punktzahl: 20

1. Apostrophe test

1. That **woman's** jacket.
2. **Bob's** daughter.
3. My **parents'** caravan.
4. **Men's** clothes.
5. A **girl's** name.
6. A **woman's** bicycle.
7. A **boys'** school.
8. A **bird's** nest.
9. Last **night's** game.
10. **Yesterday's** paper.
11. A **year's** salary.
12. A **minute's** silence.
13. Two **hours'** sleep.
14. The **company's** HQ.
15. The **world's** population.
16. The **girls'** club.
17. **Holland's** largest city.

18. A **woman's** hat.
19. Next **week's** meeting
20. A good **night's** sleep.

Gesamtpunktzahl ______ **/20**

Weniger als 10 Punkte	11–15 Punkte	16–19 Punkte	20 Punkte
Wenn jemand ein Apostroph nicht von einem Semikolon unterscheiden kann … Versuch es noch einmal!	Muss mehr drin sein, oder?	Nicht schlecht. Gib alles, um noch besser zu werden!	Ausgezeichnet! Das Apostroph verbirgt keine Geheimnisse mehr.

Point 9 – Progress test
Know your articles

Maximale Punktzahl: 30

1. The & a/an test

1. b. I want to study at **Cologne University**.
2. a. They put up **a united front** and won their case.
3. b. We had to wait for over **an hour** for the bus.
4. a. I saw Swan Lake at **the Royal Albert Hall**.
5. a. I don't believe it, she's got **red hair**!
6. b. I don't like walking in **Hyde Park**.
7. a. I don't like walking in **the park**.
8. a. I saw **a unicorn** yesterday.

9. b.	There now follows **a history** of American culture, the programme will last approximately 16 seconds.
10. a.	I have just seen **a one-legged man**.

Punktzahl ____ /10

2. Choose the correct article

1. **an** egg
2. **an** uncle
3. **a** United player
4. **a** friend
5. **a** university
6. **a** white horse
7. **a** house
8. **an** eskimo
9. **a** union
10. **a** one-man show
11. **a** hotel
12. **an** ice cream
13. **a** helmet
14. **an** hourly rate
15. **a** hope
16. **an** idiot
17. **an** acorn
18. **an** umbrella
19. **an** apple
20. **an** eagle

Punktzahl ____ /20

Gesamtpunktzahl		
1.		
2.		
Total		/30

Weniger als 20 Punkte	20–23 Punkte	24–27 Punkte	Über 28 Punkte
Ach je. *A* oder *an* Katastrophe! Zurückspulen und wiederholen.	Zu durchschnittlich, um gut zu sein.	Gut, aber ist es gut genug?	Ausgezeichnet! Wer braucht schon ein Grammatikbuch?

Point 10 – Progress test
Be positive about negatives

Maximale Punktzahl: 20

1. Weekend shopping

I **don't** like shopping. But every Saturday I go into town with my mother to do the weekly grocery shop. She **doesn't** like shopping. It **doesn't** take long to drive into town, about 10 minutes. I **don't** like parking in the big, multi-storey carpark, so we leave my car in one of the side streets, the parking is cheaper there too.

I **can't** stand the crowds in the market and in the stores, but it **doesn't** seem to bother my mother. Last week we **didn't** go shopping together because my mother was ill. She **doesn't** like missing out on our weekly get-together.

Next weekend, we are **not** going shopping because my mother is going on a trip with her friends. I am **not** going shopping on my own, so I can enjoy a nice, relaxing morning at home.

Punktzahl ______ **/10**

2. Choose the correct negative

1. I like meat, but I **don't like** fish.
2. My dad eats fish, but he **doesn't eat** chicken.
3. I am **not watching** the news.
4. My parents **don't listen** to the radio.
5. I **haven't finished** my homework yet.
6. Paul **hasn't woken up** yet.
7. I **wasn't early** for work today.
8. She **doesn't listen** to a word I say.
9. My maths teacher **doesn't give** homework at the weekend.
10. We are **not saving** money for a house.

Punktzahl ______ **/10**

Gesamtpunktzahl	
1.	
2.	
Total	/20

Weniger als 14 Punkte	14–16 Punkte	17–19 Punkte	20 Punkte
Ein sehr negatives Ergebnis. Versuch es noch einmal.	Negativ durchschnittlich.	Mehr positiv als negativ!	Ausgezeichnet! *Positively brillant!*

Point 11 – Progress test Don't confuse your words

Maximale Punktzahl: 30

1. Confusing words

1. I picked up my **prescription**.
2. My plane was **delayed** by an hour.
3. Never **borrow** money from a friend.
4. We always **check** each delivery.
5. Paul will be arriving **shortly**.
6. You really shouldn't read **confidential** documents.
7. I sometimes talk **aloud**.
8. He was **bare** when he opened the door.
9. **It's** time to go.
10. You're very **quiet**? Is something bothering you?

11. We had to **queue** for ages.
12. I **hardly** know Bob.
13. Tom works **hard**.
14. It's on the fifth **storey**.
15. He **passed** the test.

16 I am going to see the **principal**.

17. He works on a building **site**.
18. There is a terrible **draught** in here.
19. They fitted a water **meter** in our kitchen.
20. An **altar** is part of a church.
21. The **brakes** on my car don't work.
22. I usually have **cereal** for breakfast.
23. I don't like him, he's rather **coarse**.
24. Ask Bob, he'll **lend** you some money.
25. I made an **appointment** with the doctor.
26. Are you putting **currants** in that cake?
27. She broke her ankle, she fell over the **kerb**.
28. A specialist has agreed to **counsel** her.
29. Paul **complimented** me.
30. Did you **lose** the game?

Gesamtpunktzahl ______ /30

Weniger als 15 Punkte	**15–20 Punkte**	**21–29 Punkte**	**30 Punkte**
Verwirrt genug, um diesen Abschnitt noch einmal zu machen …	Halb verwirrt. Mehr Konzentration benötigt.	Gut, aber immer noch Luft nach oben.	Herzlichen Glückwünsch. Hier ist kein Platz für Verwirrung.

Point 12 – Progress test
Avoid Denglish (Get to know your false friends)

Maximale Punktzahl: 20

1. False friends

1. I don't like his **art**.	**style**
2. I **became** a new bicycle for Christmas.	**got**
3. My new **chef** is not very nice.	**boss**
4. Who is your **actual** girlfriend?	**current**
5. I made a lot of **failures** in my exams.	**mistakes**
6. My new **handy** has got a camera.	**mobile**
7. He is easily offended, he is very **sensible**.	**sensitive**
8. They put a label on the **backside**.	**back**
9. The English **kitchen** isn't very good.	**cuisine/food**
10. They got lost in the **dessert** and died after five days.	**desert**
11. I bought a new **objective** for my camera.	**lens**
12. Always **proof** your car tyres before a long journey.	**check**
13. RTL **sent** a great programme about birds last night.	**broadcast**
14. Everyone likes him, he's such a **sympathetic** guy.	**nice**
15. The hotel is too **wide** to walk, take a taxi.	**far**
16. I do not need your **rat**.	**advice**
17. Our **travel** to Kenya was fascinating.	**trip**
18. We have a shortage of **personal**.	**personnel**
19. I **spent** €50 to Oxfam.	**donated**
20. Sally works in a **fabric**.	**factory**

Gesamtpunktzahl ____ **/20**

Weniger als 12 Punkte	13–16 Punkte	17–19 Punkte	20 Punkte
Falsche Freunde sind keine Freunde. Noch ein Versuch?	Viele dieser falschen Freunde waren illusorisch. Versuch es noch einmal!	Gut, fast da, aber nicht ganz!	Großartig! Falsche Freunde sind kein Feind!

Point 13 – Progress test Widen your vocabulary

Maximale Punktzahl: 20

1. One word – two meanings

1. The game ended in a **draw.**	**unentschieden**/zeichnen
2. Can you **iron** my shirt, please?	**bügeln**/eisern
3. I am trying hard to **save** money.	retten/**sparen**
4. Are you going to midnight **mass**?	**Gottesdienst**/Menge
5. I wrote my number on a **slip** of paper.	**Zettel**/rutschen
6. Did you **join** the fitness club?	Verbinden/**eintreten**
7. They offer third-**class** service.	Klasse/**Rang**
8. Have you got the **key** to the caravan?	Tonart/**Schlüssel**
9. Did you **log** on?	Holzklotz/**registrieren**
10. When did you **break** that vase?	**brechen**/Pause

Punktzahl ______ **/10**

2. Words that sound the same but are written differently

1. A line of people or vehicles.	**queue**
2. A breakfast food made from grains.	**cereal**
3. Having two parts.	**dual**
4. Happening now.	**current**
5. A Middle Eastern market.	**bazaar**
6. A group of musical notes.	**chord**
7. A long, slender piece of wood.	**pole**
8. To stop a vehicle.	**brake**
9. Rough.	**coarse**
10. A sacred table in a church.	**altar**

Punktzahl ____ **/10**

Gesamtpunktzahl		
1.		
2.		
Total		**/20**

Weniger als 12 Punkte	**13–16 Punkte**	**17–19 Punkte**	**20 Punkte**
	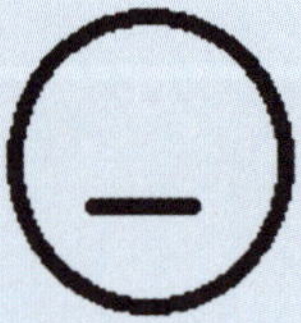		

Point 14 – Progress test
Get to know your silent letters

Maximale Punktzahl: 15

1. Odd man out

1. climb	comb	doubt	el**b**ow
2. hour	exhaust	exhibition	in**h**ale
3. column	hymn	autumn	hyphe**n**
4. **k**ill	know	knot	knife
5. swords	answer	s**w**ing	write
6. wa**d**e	handsome	Wednesday	grandson
7. guest	guilt	tongue	lang**u**age
8. island	gra**s**p	isle	Illinois
9. receipt	psychology	pneumonia	**p**etal
10. who**l**e	salmon	half	calm
11. **w**elcome	write	wren	two
12. fasten	listen	castle	ta**s**te
13. biscuit	**u**nder	tongue	guard
14. sin**g**	sign	design	foreigner
15. would	should	co**l**our	could

Gesamtpunktzahl ____ /15

Weniger als 10 Punkte	10–11 Punkte	12–14 Punkte	15 Punkte
Schweigen ist nicht Gold. Schau es noch einmal an.	Es ist schwer, die Stille zu sehen, oder?	Gut, fast da!	Großartig!

Point 15 – Progress test
Understand the will future

Maximale Punktzahl: 10

1. Will future

1. You have plans to meet your girlfriend in the city tonight.
   I **am meeting** Sue tonight.
2. You and your friend have booked a holiday in Italy next summer.
   We **are going** to Italy in July.
3. You might go to the cinema tonight, but you are not sure.
   Maybe **I will go** to the cinema tonight.
4. You are moving to Spain in three months.
   I **am moving** to Spain in three months.
5. Your partner comes home, cold and hungry.
   I **will make** you something to eat.
6. You meet your neighbour, his car has broken down.
   He needs to get to the city urgently.
   I **will give** you a lift into the city.
7. You might go to Portugal for Christmas
   I **might go** to Portugal for Christmas.
8. You have plans to play football on Sunday with some old friends.
   I **am playing** football at the weekend.
9. You will probably watch the big tonight.
   I **might watch** the big game tonight.
10. You have decided to paint the kitchen at the weekend.
    I **am painting** the kitchen at the weekend.

Gesamtpunktzahl ____ **/10**

5 Punkte oder weniger	6–7 Punkte	8–9 Punkte	10 Punkte
›Will‹ hat diesmal gewonnen … Schau es nochmal an.	Wo ein Wille ist, ist auch ein Weg … um besser zu werden!	Wird (will) die oberste Ebene erreicht werden?	Einfach wunderbar!

Point 16 – Progress test Colour your English

Maximale Punktzahl: 10

1. Colour your English

1. ›Taking the mickey‹ means

   a. Making fun of someone

2. ›Yellow‹ means:

   b. Afraid

3. ›Done up like a kipper‹ means:

   b. Fooled

4. ›You are pulling my leg‹ means:

   b. You are joking with me

5. ›Hit the sack‹ means:

   a. Go to bed

6. A ›hot potato‹ is:

   b. A tricky subject

7. ›Fall off the back of a lorry‹ means:

   a. Stolen

8. ›Do a runner‹ means:

   b. Run off without paying

9. ›For donkey's years‹ means:
   a. A long time

10. ›To bend over backwards‹ means:
   b. To be very helpful

Gesamtpunktzahl /10

5 Punkte oder weniger	6–7 Punkte	8–9 Punkte	10 Punkte
Hoppla! Idioms sind eine heiße Kartoffel für manche Leute!	Man muss sich nach hinten beugen, um besser zu werden …	Don't throw a wobbly, es ist ein gutes Ergebnis!	Toll! *Time to get ›blotto‹*!

Point 17 – Progress test Use better words

Maximale Punktzahl: 20

1. Advanced adverbs

1. He was **terribly** injured.
2. The roof was **badly** damaged.
3. He is **awfully** selfish.
4. She is **unbelievably** shy.
5. She is **heavily** pregnant.
6. The weather was **extremely** hot.
7. My hotel was **incredibly** expensive.

8. The meeting was **fairly** useful.
9. He was **pleasantly** surprised.
10. My flight was **slightly** delayed.

Punktzahl ____ /10

2. Prefixes

1. Many politicians are very **unprofessional**.
2. He doesn't make a lot of sense, he's **illogical**.
3. She is chaotic and extremely **disorganised**.
4. I was **unaware** of any problems.
5. I think ›teach' is an **irregular** verb.
6. Tom is always so **impatient**.
7. She is very childish and **immature**.
8. Those terms are totally **unacceptable** to me.
9. He is not a good speaker, rather **inarticulate**.
10. She was **unwilling** to compromise.

Punktzahl ____ /10

Gesamtpunktzahl		
1.		
2.		
Total		/20

10 Punkte oder weniger	11–13 Punkte	14–19 Punkte	20 Punkte
Es gibt einen Unterschied zwischen Adverbien und Adjektiven!	Etwas mehr als die Hälfte. Das geht besser …	Gut, aber nicht super.	Fantastisch! Perfektion!

Point 18 – Progress test
Avoid making the biggest mistakes
Maximale Punktzahl: 30

1. Avoid making the biggest mistakes

1. Tom **said** he was really tired.
2. Don't **tell** me, let me guess.
3. John **is sitting** in a chair.
4. Eric **plays** cricket every Saturday.
5. Last week I **went** to Holland.
6. I **have** been to Africa.
7. I like **reading**.
8. I love **cooking**.
9. I hate **paying** tax.
10. I don't mind **cleaning**.
11. Did you **watch** the game last night?
12. Do you **watch** sport on TV?
13. He said the gold was **real**.
14. That is simply not **true**.
15. I like **listening** to **classical** music.
16. It is **normal** to cheat the taxman.
17. Paul doesn't **normally** drink alcohol.

18. Be **careful**.
19. He is **extremely** unhappy.
20. He was **really** shocked.
21. Are you **interested** sport?
22. Do you find politics **interesting**?
23. Just follow my **instructions**.
24. Sorry, but I don't **agree** with you.
25. There is **a** big hotel in the centre.
26. I am proud to be **a** European.
27. Sue is married to **an** African.
28. The pound is **a** unit of currency.
29. There is **a** university in the city.
30. He was **an** old man.

Gesamtpunktzahl ____ **/30**

Unter 20 Punkte	**20–25 Punkte**	**26–29 Punkte**	**30 Punkte**
Die Fehler wurden nicht vermieden. Versuch es noch einmal!	Zu viele Fehler wurden nicht vermieden.	Die meisten Fehler wurden gefunden. Fast perfekt!	Toll. Gut gemacht!

Point 19 – Progress test
Make better small talk

Maximale Punktzahl: 20

1. Make better small talk

1. What do you do for a **living**?
2. Can you speak **slowly**?
3. **Would you** like something to drink?
4. Where **are** you from?
5. How was your **journey**?
6. Are there any side **effects**?
7. Pleased to **meet** you.
8. How do you say ›please' in **German**?
9. I'm **bored**.
10. It was nice **meeting** you.
11. I'm not **interested**!
12. I'm **married**.
13. I'm **hungry**.
14. Hurry **up**!
15. I **don't** understand.
16. In which hotel are you **staying**?
17. I would like to **invite** you for dinner.
18. I don't **drink** alcohol.
19. Pleased to **see** you again.
20. My **German** is bad.

Gesamtpunktzahl ____ /20

Unter 10 Punkte	10–15 Punkte	16–19 Punkte	20 Punkte
Ach je! Keine Reisepläne, hoffe ich …	Diese Art von Small Talk muss mehr werden.	Gut genug vorbereitet, um Smalltalk zu treiben.	Chatten nach Herzenslust. Kein Problem!

Point 20
Abschlusstest

Maximale Punktzahl: 40

1. Abschlusstest

1. Time **flies**.
2. It's **defect**.
3. I **am having** a party on Saturday.
4. Paul **is going** to a party now.
5. He **does** a lot of business with Japan.
6. **Have you** ever swum in the ocean?
7. **Have you** ever driven a sports car?
8. Where **do** your parents live?
9. **Is** Paul coming to the party?
10. Two **tomatoes**.
11. Two **buses**.
12. Five **sheep**.
13. Two **wives**.
14. Making mistakes is really **frustrating**.
15. I get **frustrated** when I can't express myself.
16. **Take off** your coat.
17. I am not afraid **of** snakes.
18. He rides **on** his horse.

19. She got married **at** 18.
20. **Yesterday's** paper.
21. A **year's** salary.
22. A **minute's** silence.
23. I like walking in **Hyde Park**.
24. I don't like walking in **the park**.
25. I picked up my **prescription**.
26. My plane was **delayed** by an hour.
27. Never **borrow** money from a friend.
28. We always **check** each delivery.
29. The English **cuisine** isn't very good.
30. They got lost in the **desert** and died.
31. Always **check** your car tyres regularly.
32. Maybe **I will** go to the cinema tonight.
33. I **am moving** to Spain in three months.
34. Yellow means: **afraid**
35. Blotto means: **drunk**
36. I like **reading**.
37. I love **cooking**.
38. I hate **paying** tax.
39. I hurt **myself**.
40. It's **terribly** expensive.

Gesamtpunktzahl ____ /40

Unter 30 Punkte	30–34 Punkte	35–39 Punkte	40 Punkte
Hat da jemand während der letzten 20 Kapitel geschlafen?	Ein oder zwei Kapitel sollten überprüft werden.	Fast brillant!	Großartig! Dein Englisch ist jetzt offiziell hervorragend!